ATLAS of FOOTBALL

Discover the world of the beautiful game

First published in Great Britain 2018 by Red Shed,
an imprint of Egmont UK Limited
The Yellow Building, 1 Nicholas Road, London W11 4AN

www.egmont.co.uk

Text copyright © Egmont UK Limited 2018

Illustrations copyright © Tracy Worrall 2018

ISBN 978 1 4052 8726 5

Cartographic consultancy by Lynn Neal.

A CIP catalogue record for this book is available from the British Library.

Stay safe online. Any website addresses listed in this book are correct at the time
of going to print. However, Egmont is not responsible for content hosted
by third parties. Please be aware that online content can be subject to
change and websites can contain content that is unsuitable for children.
We advise that all children are supervised when using the internet.

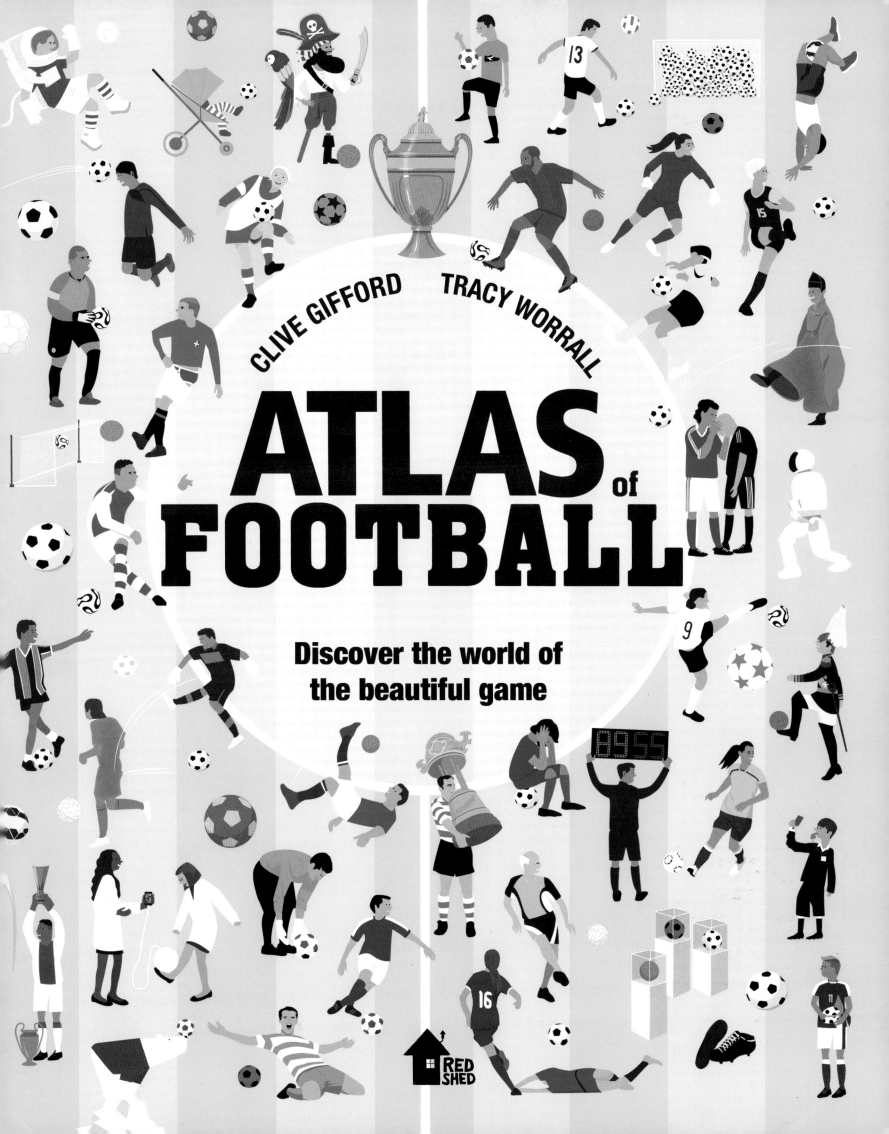

CLIVE GIFFORD · TRACY WORRALL

ATLAS of FOOTBALL

Discover the world of the beautiful game

RED SHED

CONTENTS

ITALY
pp24–25

ARCTIC OCEAN

CENTRAL AND
EASTERN EUROPE
pp28–29

EASTERN
MEDITERRANEAN
pp26–27

NORTHERN ASIA
pp68–69

CENTRAL ASIA
pp70–71

EASTERN ASIA
pp74–75

PACIFIC OCEAN

INDIAN
SUBCONTINENT
p72

SOUTHERN ASIA
p73

INDIAN OCEAN

PACIFIC ISLANDS
p83

AUSTRALIA AND
PAPUA NEW GUINEA
pp80–81

NEW ZEALAND
p82

SOUTHERN OCEAN

ANTARCTICA

INTRODUCTION

NORTH AMERICA

PACIFIC OCEAN

ATLANTIC OCEAN

Discover Aqsaqtuk, a version of football played on snow and ice for centuries.

Admire the flamboyant fashions of Mexican goalkeeper Jorge Campos.

Football is the world's most popular team sport, played by hundreds of millions and watched by hundreds of millions more. The game grips spectators like no other, with its rich traditions and the rivalries between passionate fans of both clubs and national teams.

Football is played by and enjoyed in every nation in the world, from indoor arena matches and beach football on scenic shorelines to casual games crammed into crowded city streets or rooftop pitches on tall city buildings.

Follow football's phenomenal growth and popularity with this incredible round the world adventure. As you travel from region to region, you'll get to grips with the competitions, traditions, star players, coaches and teams of different countries. Find out how the game developed, and revel in the funny and extraordinary moments and events that make football so popular everywhere.

SO, KICK OFF YOUR FOOTBALLING JOURNEY, AND SEE THE WORLD IN A WHOLE NEW LIGHT!

SOUTH AMERICA

Try to beat Brazilian Milene Dominguez's world record for keeping a football in the air.

Wonder at the unveiling of a World Cup logo from the International Space Station.

ARCTIC OCEAN

Check out Finnish second division club FC Santa Claus.

Drop in at Russia's first-ever public museum of football in Samara.

EUROPE

Learn about Romanian Adrian Mutu's strange pre-match superstitions.

ASIA

Watch a US president play football with a robot, in Tokyo, Japan.

Visit the largest football in the world in Doha, Qatar.

AFRICA

PACIFIC OCEAN

Witness Manoj Mishra balance a ball on his head while riding a motorcycle in West Bengal.

OCEANIA

INDIAN OCEAN

Meet the competitive football playing grannies of Limpopo Province, South Africa.

Find out what happens when a football game is interrupted by a charging bull.

Watch professionals playing football at the coldest place on Earth.

ANTARCTICA

EUROPE

ICELAND

ATLANTIC OCEAN

IRELAND

UNITED KINGDOM

NORTH SEA

NETHERLAND

BELGIUM

LUXEMBOURG

BAY OF BISCAY

FRANCE

SWITZERLA

ANDORRA

PORTUGAL

SPAIN

This continent is the most powerful and successful in the global game. Half of all the World Cup tournaments have been held here and 11 of the first 20 winners were European.

The Union of European Football Associations (UEFA) was formed in 1954 to govern football in Europe. It has 55 members including several countries, such as Russia and Armenia, who geographically span both Europe and Asia. UEFA runs the European Championships, as well as the UEFA Champions League – the biggest competition for football clubs in the world.

Boosted by the Champions League, the top European clubs have become very rich and are able to attract the finest footballers from around the world to play for them and thrill the fans.

```
0        250        500 miles
0    250     500 kilometres
```

BARENTS SEA

NORWEGIAN
SEA

SWEDEN

FINLAND

NORWAY

RUSSIA
Sits in both
Europe and Asia

ESTONIA

LATVIA

DENMARK

BALTIC
SEA

LITHUANIA

KALININGRAD
Part of Russia

BELARUS

ERMANY

POLAND

CZECH
REPUBLIC

SLOVAKIA

UKRAINE

ECHTENSTEIN

AUSTRIA

MOLDOVA

HUNGARY

CASPIAN
SEA

SLOVENIA

CROATIA

ROMANIA

BOSNIA AND
HERZEGOVINA

SERBIA

BLACK SEA

MONTENEGRO KOSOVO

BULGARIA

ITALY

MACEDONIA

ALBANIA

TURKEY
Sits in both
Europe and Asia

GREECE

MALTA

CYPRUS

MEDITERRANEAN SEA

13. EIDI

The Við Margáir football ground in the Faroe Islands is exposed on two sides to the Atlantic Ocean. When the ball leaves the pitch, staff or supporters often have to go out in a rowing boat to retrieve it!

TÓRSHAVN

13

Flekkeroy IL football club bought striker Kenneth Kristensen from Vindbjart in 2002 for an unusual transfer fee – the player's weight in prawns! Kristensen was weighed in at 75kg!

BARENTS SEA

10. TROMSØ

Playing at the Alfheim Stadion deep within the Arctic Circle, Tromsø IL are the most northerly top flight professional football club in the world. The official supporters of this chilly club are called Isberget ('the Iceberg') and have a polar bear as their logo and mascot.

10

When midfielder Stefan Schwarz moved to English club Sunderland in 1999, his contract banned him from ever travelling into space! In interviews beforehand, Schwarz had said he would love to travel on a spacecraft.

3. ROVANIEMI

This city on the edge of the Arctic Circle is home to Finland second division club FC Santa Claus. Founded in 1993, the club plays in red and white, and their club crest features Santa Claus!

3

2. HYRYNSALMI

The Swamp Soccer World Championships are held here every year. More than 200 teams, with six players a side, contest games played on 6m-long patches of muddy swamp.

Swedish footballer Hans Jeppson was the world's most expensive footballer in 1952, when he was bought by Italian club, Napoli, for £52,000. Jeppson was the first European player outside the UK to achieve such a sum.

Torneälven river

NORWEGIAN SEA

2

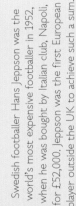

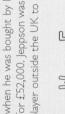

S W E D E N

N O R W A Y

NORWEGIAN SEA

100 miles

100 kilometres

I C E L A N D

In 2011, Hannes Þór Halldórsson made his debut in goal for the Icelandic national team. The following year, he directed the video for Iceland's entry into the 2012 Eurovision Song Contest. Halldórsson has also directed adverts and short movies.

REYKJAVIK

12

12. GARÐABÆR

Ungmennafélagið Stjarnan caused an internet sensation in 2010. Each time the team scored, the players would act out an elaborate mime, such as catching a fish, diving into a swimming pool or forming a moving human bicycle.

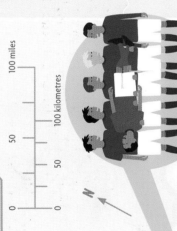

100 miles

100 kilometres

11. VESTMANNAEYJAR

In 1973, an erupting volcano covered the pitch of Íþróttabandalag Vestmannaeyja (ÍBV) in red hot lava! The team did not get their ground back for several years, but then went on to become Icelandic league champions three times.

11

The 1958 World Cup, hosted by Sweden, was the first held in Scandinavia. It is the only World Cup held in Europe that was not won by a European team and the only time that the four nations of the United Kingdom all qualified and took part. The tournament was notable for Pelé's arrival in world football and the Brazilian striker became the youngest goal scorer and World Cup winner.

ASIA

EUROPE

AFRICA

F I N L A N D

1. LAHTI

Jari Litmanen made his professional debut for Reipas, based in Lahti, in 1987. He notched up 137 caps for Finland, and to date is the only footballer to have played for his country in four different decades.

HELSINKI ★

Born in Malmo, the maverick Swedish striker **ZLATAN IBRAHIMOVIĆ** has won **11 LEAGUE CHAMPIONSHIPS** with clubs in the Netherlands, Spain, Italy and France. He is Sweden's all-time **LEADING SCORER** with **62 GOALS**, and he scored **38 GOALS** in just **31 GAMES** for Paris Saint-Germain in 2015–6, including the league's **FASTEST-EVER HAT-TRICK** (9 minutes). He now plays for **MANCHESTER UNITED**.

GULF OF BOTHNIA

BALTIC SEA

4. SOLNA

In 2003, Nicole Petignat became the first female referee to take charge of a UEFA Cup match when she officiated the game between Swedish club AIK Fotboll, located in Solna, and Fylkir from Iceland.

★ **STOCKHOLM**
④

EURO 1992 was the first tournament to feature shirts that had players' names as well as their numbers on the back.

Österdalälven river

Glomma river

5. BRØNDBY

Peter Schmeichel won four Danish league championships in five seasons for Brøndby, before moving to Manchester United, and is the most capped Danish player, appearing 129 times. Both he and his son, Kaspar, also a goalkeeper, have won the English Premier League.

6. MALMÖ

A five-a-side football pitch is named Zlatan Court after Swedish star striker Zlatan Ibrahimović, who used to play there as a child. The artificial pitch is made of recycled trainers and football boots.

9. TRONDHEIM
⑨

In the 1970s, Rosenborg BK defender Svein Grøndalen went out for a training jog in a nearby forest, but injured himself by colliding with a moose! Grøndalen had to withdraw from an international match for Norway, but did play 77 times for his country.

OSLO ★

Henrik Elvestad and Johan Golden invented a new twist on football in Oslo in 2011. In bubble soccer, players are encased in blow-up balls and bump and bash each other as they compete for the ball. The sport now has competitions in Europe and North America.

8. NØRAGER

Danish referee Henning Erikstrup went to blow the final whistle at a 1960 match between Nørager and Ebeltoft and lost his false teeth! As he tried to put them back in, Ebeltoft equalised to make the scoreline 4–4, but the referee disallowed the goal.

⑧

N O R T H
S E A

D E N M A R K ⑤ ⑦

COPENHAGEN ★
⑦ ⑥

7. HVIDOVRE

Danish goalkeeper Michael Stensgaard left Hvidovre IF for Liverpool in 1994, but returned to the Danish club two years later. He had left the sport due to injury – he damaged his shoulder while trying to fold an ironing board!

SCANDINAVIA

The most northerly part of Europe has a long football history. Two Danish teams played a friendly match in Sweden in 1890 around the same time that football first reached Turku in Finland. Sweden and Norway contested their first international game in 1908, and Sweden hosted both a World Cup (1958) and European Championship (1992), the latter won by Denmark. Norway are the only national football team to have never lost to Brazil.

0   50   100 miles

0   50   100 kilometres

UK AND IRELAND

England is where the modern game of association football began. It developed in the 19th century out of various unruly kicking and rushing ball games that had been played for centuries. England's oldest surviving football club, Sheffield FC, was founded in 1857. Scotland's oldest club still in existence is Queen's Park, founded in 1867. The first international match was played between England and Scotland in 1872, with Wales playing their first international four years later. From 1882 to 1921, a combined Ireland team also took part.

ASIA
EUROPE
AFRICA

SHETLAND ISLANDS

NORTH SEA

ORKNEY ISLANDS

ATLANTIC OCEAN

S C O T L A N D

EDINBURGH

100 miles

100 kilometres

50

50

0

0

1. STIRLING

During renovations at Stirling Castle in the 1970s, an ancient football was found behind panelling in the Queen's bedchamber. The ball, a pig's bladder covered in stitched pieces of cow leather, is thought to date from 1540 or even earlier, making it the oldest surviving football in the world.

The very first women's international match played by British teams was at Ravenscraig Stadium in Greenock, Renfrewshire, in 1972, when England defeated Scotland 3–2. The match was held in the same year that the FA lifted the ban on women's football games, which had been in force since 1921, and was played at a football league ground.

2. ARBROATH

When he was playing away at Arbroath in 1935, Queen of the South goalkeeper Willie Fotheringham left his false teeth in the back of his goal and forgot to pick them up. A fish delivery truck from Arbroath carried the teeth back to the goalie the following week!

3. GLASGOW

During a 1995 Scottish Premier League game between Rangers and Hibernian, referee Dougie Smith dropped his yellow card. Rangers' attacker Paul Gascoigne picked it up and jokingly booked the referee. The ref did not think it was funny and booked Gascoigne, who picked up a two-game ban as a result. At least Rangers won the match 7–0!

4. TOBERMORE

Rejected by his local club, Glentoran, for being too small, George Best joined Manchester United at the age of 15 and scored more than 200 goals for clubs all over the world, including Tobermore United, which was the only Northern Irish club he played for. In 2006, one million five pound notes

£5
GEORGE BEST
£5

5. SUNDERLAND

During their 2009 English Premier League game, a Liverpool fan threw a red beach ball on to the pitch. Sunderland striker Darren Bent struck a shot that bounced off the beach ball in the penalty area and deflected past the Liverpool goalkeeper, Pepe Reina, into the net. The goal

In 2014, an entire football club was sold on eBay for just £45! The online ad for Letchworth Albion FC stated that the club possessed 'a general lack of footballing talent' – it had only kept four clean sheets in four seasons. The club was bought by Mathew Morris and Grant Whittaker, two of its players.

6. HULL

To celebrate Hull City reaching the final of the 2014 FA Cup, some unusual memorabilia went on sale to fans, including a toilet seat in the club colours (black and gold) with the face of manager, Steve Bruce, under the lid!

A Norwegian couple who are avid Liverpool fans named their baby daughter Karoline YNWA. The YNWA is short for You'll Never Walk Alone – the song sung by Liverpool fans before every match.

7. DERBY

The first public football match on roller skates was held at the Alexandra Skating Rink in Derby in 1883. The sport developed into a five-a-side game known as roller soccer, and 120 years later the first Rollersoccer World Cup was held in London and won by the Netherlands.

★ **LONDON**

E N G L A N D

The first Wembley Stadium opened in 1923 and hosted the 1966 World Cup final (which England won), and the final of EURO 96. In 2007, it was replaced by a new stadium that holds 90,000 fans and has 2,618 toilets – more than any other stadium in the world. It cost £798 million to build and its 315m-long arch stands 133m tall at its highest point.

A new sport, Foot Darts, was unveiled in 2016 by Kent company Foot Sports Ltd. A 7m-tall inflatable dartboard is covered with a special material that allows Velcro-covered footballs to stick to it. Players score points by kicking the ball into the scoring zones just like they would when throwing darts.

ENGLISH CHANNEL

8. HOLT

This was the birthplace of Leigh Richmond Roose, an eccentric goalkeeper who played for Wales 24 times. He often performed gymnastics using the crossbar during breaks in play.

W A L E S

CELTIC SEA

★ **CARDIFF**

This is the birthplace of Gareth Bale, who played for Cardiff Civil Service before turning professional for Southampton and Tottenham Hotspur. In 2013, he moved to Spanish giants, Real Madrid, for a record fee of £85.1 million! Bale is known for his pace – at the tender age of 14, he ran 100m in 11.4 seconds.

10. SCILLY ISLES

Woolpack Wanderers and Garrison Gunners are the only teams in the world's smallest football league. Since 2012, they have joined forces to form a single team to play against Dynamo Chough from Cornwall. The winners are awarded the Lyonesse Cup – the world's tiniest football trophy at just 6mm tall.

DOUGLAS ★

ISLE OF MAN ★

IRISH SEA

Dublin-born striker Robbie Keane is the Republic of Ireland's highest goal scorer (68) and has made the most appearances (146) for his country. Keane is the only player in the world to have scored at least one international goal every season for 18 seasons in a row (1998–2016).

REPUBLIC OF IRELAND

DUBLIN ★

9. SCREGGAN

Tractor football matches are played at the National Ploughing Championships here. Three tractors per side contest each game, which is played with a 2-m diameter football. The tractors try to nudge the ball into a goal that has posts made of bales of hay.

In the 1860s, Joseph Hudson began to manufacture whistles which were first used by police forces and, a little later, football referees. By the year 2000, the company had sold over 200 million Acme Thunderer whistles, many used to stop and start football matches all over the world.

Newton Heath LYR football club changed their name in 1902 to **MANCHESTER UNITED**. Their longest serving manager was **SIR ALEX FERGUSON**. During his **26.5 YEARS** and **1,500 GAMES**, the team won the English Premier League **13 TIMES**, as well as **5 FA CUPS** and **2 UEFA** Champions League titles.

13. LENS

The first brothers to play against each other at a UEFA European Championships were Granit Xhaka, who played for Switzerland, and his older brother, Taulant, who played for Albania. The pair faced up to each other at Euro 2016 and Switzerland won 1–0.

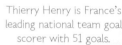

Thierry Henry is France's leading national team goal scorer with 51 goals.

12. RENNES

The son of an Angolan mother and a member of Zaire's 1974 World Cup football team, Rio Mavuba was born in a boat off the coast of Angola in 1984. His birth certificate does not list a nationality, simply stating 'Born at sea'. After playing club football in France and Spain, Mavuba made his debut for the French national football team in Rennes in 2004.

PARIS ★

Thierry Henry was just 13 when a scout watched him play for Paris's ES Viry-Châtillon. Henry's team won 6–0 and he scored all six goals! In total, he scored 77 goals in 26 matches for the club.

11. AUXERRE

GAME NO. 2,000

In 1961, 22-year-old Guy Roux became manager of AJ Auxerre for a season. Then, in 1964, he returned as manager and stayed in charge for more than 36 years! Under his guidance for over 2,000 games, the club won their first ever French league title in 1996.

BAY OF BISCAY

10. CLERMONT-FERRAND

Helena Costa was made head coach of men's Ligue 2 football team, Clermont Foot 63, in 2014. She had formerly been in charge of Iran's national women's team, before becoming the first female coach in French men's professional football.

MASSIF CENTRAL

9. TOULOUSE

At the 1998 World Cup, French defender Laurent Blanc's pre-match ritual saw him kiss the bald head of his teammate, goalkeeper, Fabien Barthez. It must have worked as France won the tournament!

PYRENEES

8. MARSEILLE

Just as he was about to take a crucial penalty in the 1938 World Cup semi-final, Italian Giuseppe Meazza's shorts fell down! Despite the sniggers of the opposing team, Brazil, Meazza held up his shorts with one hand as he ran and scored the winning goal. Italy went on to win the World Cup in Paris.

Super Victor was unveiled in 2014 as the mascot of the 2016 UEFA European Championships (EURO 2016). A boy with a cape and footballing superpowers, his name was chosen by an internet vote, beating the alternatives, Driblou and Goalix.

The first European Championships was held in France in 1960. It cost national teams just 100 Swiss Francs (around £50) to enter. At Euro 2016, teams were paid instead of paying to enter. They received a minimum of €8 million, with the tournament winners, Portugal, earning over €25 million.

0   100   200 miles

0   100   200 kilometres

1. LILLE

France's EURO 2016 match versus Switzerland at the Stade Pierre-Mauroy saw several rare equipment failures. The shirts of three Swiss players all ripped badly and when Swiss midfielder Valon Behrami went to kick the ball, it burst!

2. METZ

FC Metz rejected Michel Platini in 1971 after he fainted during a breathing test. The talented midfielder went on to play for Nancy, St Etienne and Juventus, and scored 41 goals for the French national team. His nine goals at EURO 1984 remain a competition record.

3. THEULEY-LES-LAVONCOURT

Jules Rimet was born in his father's grocery store here in 1873. He went on to found both France's first national football league and, later, the FIFA World Cup. He carried the World Cup trophy in his bag when he sailed to Uruguay in 1930 for the first competition (*see 7, below*).

4. SAINT-VIT

This was the birthplace of French referee Michel Vautrot, who during the 1990 World Cup semi-final forgot to look at his watch and, as a result, caused the teams to play 23 minutes of extra time instead of just 15 minutes.

5. LYON

Founded in 1950, Olympique Lyonnais originally played in all-white shirts. In the final of the Coupe de France in 2012, part of their strip could only be seen by viewers wearing 3D glasses — a first in football history!

ALPS

MONACO

★ MONACO

7. VILLEFRANCHE-SUR-MER

The *Conte Verde* set sail from here in 1930 to take the French, Belgian and Romanian teams across the Atlantic Ocean to Uruguay to take part in the first ever FIFA World Cup. The ship picked up the Brazilian team along the way!

6. BASTIA

Sporting Club de Bastia was the first professional football club Cyril Rool played for. Known as a tough-tackling midfielder who went on to play for Monaco, Marseilles and OGC Nice, Rool notched up 25 red cards and 187 yellow cards during his career.

CORSICA

MEDITERRANEAN SEA

FRANCE

If England was the birthplace of football, then France was where it started to grow up and become a worldwide competitive sport. French football officials founded FIFA, suggested the idea of a World Cup and organised the first European Championships in 1960. France has hosted the EUROs three times, the latest in 2016, and the FIFA World Cup twice, winning it on the second occasion in 1998.

Born in Marseilles, skilful attacking midfielder **ZINEDINE ZIDANE** was voted the world's best footballer **THREE TIMES** and won both the **1998 WORLD CUP** and **EURO 2000** with France. He also won the **UEFA CHAMPIONS LEAGUE** as both a player (in 2002) and a coach (2016), both with the same team — **REAL MADRID**.

Although Monaco is an independent country, its biggest team, AS Monaco, plays in France and has won the French Ligue 1 Championship seven times. Their stadium, Stade Louis II, is small for a champion team, only holding 18,523 fans. But that still provides room for more than half of Monaco's entire population.

SPAIN AND PORTUGAL

Home to famous clubs such as Barcelona and Atlético Madrid in Spain, and Benfica and Porto in Portugal, these two countries have won the last three UEFA European Championships. Portugal hosted the competition in 2004 and Spain in 1964, while Spain won the 2010 World Cup. Spain's Real Madrid is Europe's most successful club with 11 Champions League triumphs and a record 32 La Liga league championships.

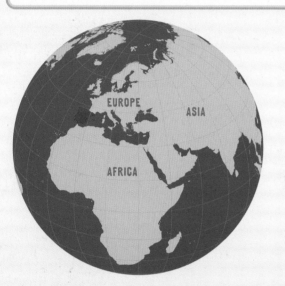

EUROPE

ASIA

AFRICA

ATLANTIC OCEAN

1. A CORUÑA

Deportivo La Coruña went 26 league games without conceding a goal during the 1993–4 season, a Spanish record. The club were the last to win La Liga, which they did for the first time in 1999–2000. They were called Turcos ('the Turks') by rivals, a name they have kept as a nickname with fans waving Turkish flags before every home game.

2. BRAGA

Braga's Estádio Municipal is chiselled into an old quarry. One end is a solid rock face and has no seats. To move from one giant side stand to another, fans have to walk through an underground passage that runs directly beneath the pitch.

3. PORTO

Portuguese coach José Mourinho's amazing 150-match run of never losing a home league match began at Porto in February 2002. It was only broken in April 2011.

4. FIGUEIRA DA FOZ

In 2006, while playing against Associação Naval 1° de Maio, Sporting Lisbon's Ronny Heberson struck the fastest free kick ever recorded. The ball reached a record speed of 211km/h – faster than the top speed of most cars!

PORTUGAL

5. CALDAS DE RAINHA

The longest continuous tournament for human table football took place at Foz do Arehlo beach here in 2004. It featured 73 teams of people who took the place of model footballers on a giant-sized table. The game lasted 24 hours.

LISBON ★

6. MONTIJO

This was the location of Ricardo Soares Pereira's first professional club. The goalkeeper helped knock England out of the Euro 2004 quarter-finals by saving a penalty in the shootout with the score at 5–5, before taking and scoring the winning penalty himself.

7. HUELVA

Recreativo de Huelva is Spain's oldest football club, founded by an English doctor in 1889. They reached the final of a major cup competition for the first time in 2003, losing in the final of the Copa del Rey to RCD Mallorca.

MADEIRA ISLANDS (PART OF PORTUGAL) IN THE ATLANTIC OCEAN, OFF THE COAST OF NORTHWESTERN AFRICA

8. FUNCHAL

Cristiano Ronaldo built a large, two-storey museum in his home town dedicated to himself! The CR7 Museum features more than 125 medals and trophies that the player has won. Close by is Hotel CR7 – a five-star luxury hotel, also built by Ronaldo.

N

MADEIRA ISLANDS

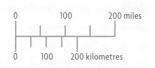

| 0 | 100 | 200 miles |
| 0 | 100 | 200 kilometres |

9. JEREZ

Santiago Cañizares, Spain's first-choice goalkeeper, missed the 2002 World Cup after injuring himself by dropping a bottle of aftershave on his foot at the Spanish team's training camp. The keeper lost his place to Iker Casillas, who went on to become the most capped Spanish player of all time, playing in more than 160 games.

0   100   200 miles

0   100   200 kilometres

14. BILBAO

Rafael Moreno Aranzadi was just 1.54m tall, but proved a lethal goal scorer in the early 20th century, despite wearing a white piece of cloth on his head to shield him from the sun. His nickname, Pichichi, is given to the trophy awarded to Spain's leading La Liga goal scorer each season.

13. HUESCA

Spain's superfan Manuel Cáceres Artesero grew up in this city and has banged a bass drum in support of Spain for over 35 years. In 1982, he hitch-hiked 15,800km to watch every single match that Spain played.

PYRENEES

A tiny nation on the France-Spain border, Andorra's national team finally won only their second competitive match in 2016, beating Macedonia 2–1 in a World Cup qualifier. The team won despite a 16-hour delay because of torrential rain. The final 14 minutes were played the next day.

ANDORRA
★ ANDORRA LA VELLA

S P A I N

12. ALAGÓN

This was the birthplace of Barcelona goalkeeper Jesús Angoy. He married the daughter of famed Dutch footballer Johan Cruyff and, in 1996, switched sports to become an American Football kicker, playing in Italy, Spain and the United States.

World Cup mascots are often based on animals, but the mascot for the 1982 World Cup, held in Spain, was an orange called Naranjito.

★ MADRID

In 2011, during a parade to celebrate a Spanish Cup win, Real Madrid defender Sergio Ramos dropped the Copa del Rey trophy, which was then run over by the open-top bus carrying the team. Whoops!

Portugal's greatest goal machine was Fernando Peyroteo. During the 1930s and 1940s, he averaged 1.6 goals scored every time he played – 540 goals in just 334 games and all for Sporting Lisbon. In a 1942 game versus Leça FC he scored nine times!

BALEARIC ISLANDS

11. ELCHE

At their 1982 World Cup Group 3 match versus El Salvador, Hungary became the first team ever to score double figures at a World Cup match, winning 10–1. Their goals included a hat-trick by László Kiss in just seven minutes, the first hat-trick by a substitute.

MEDITERRANEAN SEA

10. GIBRALTAR

Football was first played here in 1892, but it was not until 2016 that Gibraltar were admitted into FIFA and allowed to enter World Cup qualifying. In their third World Cup game, Belgium's Christian Benteke scored the fastest World Cup qualifying goal ever, striking after just 8.1 seconds in a 6–0 win.

Born in Mozambique in 1942, **EUSÉBIO DA SILVA FERREIRA** moved to Portugal as a teenager, where he starred for **BENFICA**. His **POWERFUL SHOT**, flair and thumping **HEADERS** resulted in him scoring **470 GOALS**, and winning 11 Portuguese league titles and the **1962 EUROPEAN CUP**. He also won the **GOLDEN BOOT** for the most goals (9) at the **1966 WORLD CUP**.

16. OBERHAUSEN

Paul, an octopus who lived at Oberhausen's Sea Life centre, became a celebrity during the 2010 World Cup by predicting correctly the outcome of all of Germany's seven matches at the tournament — including their defeats! He simply headed towards one of two plastic boxes bearing the national flags of whichever two teams were playing a game.

NORTH SEA

15. ALMELO

The first pitch made of artificial grass to be approved by FIFA was installed by Dutch club Heracles Almelo in 2005. A FIFA 2 Star artificial pitch like this one is allowed for UEFA Champions League and other top matches.

15

Dutch football legend **JOHAN CRUYFF** (1947–2016) led Ajax to three consecutive **EUROPEAN CUPS** (1971–3) and then guided the **NETHERLANDS** to the **WORLD CUP FINAL** in 1974. As a footballer, he scored **392 TIMES** over a **19-YEAR** career, later becoming an inspirational **COACH** and **MANAGER**.

AMSTERDAM ★

NETHERLANDS

14. BRUGES

FC Brugge have managed to qualify for the UEFA Cup or Europa League for a record 20 consecutive seasons — from 1996–7 up to and including the 2015–6 season.

14

BRUSSELS ★

BELGIUM

13 *Meuse river*

13. GENK

Football club Racing Boxberg signed Genk youngster Bryce Brites in 2013. Bryce was just 20 months old!

PRINZ 9

Rhine river

4

The innovative Stade de Suisse, in Bern, Switzerland, home to BSC Young Boys, features solar panels on its roof that generate approximately 1.2 million kilowatt hours of electricity, which is enough to power the stadium and around 400 homes close by.

LUXEMBOURG

LUXEMBOURG ★

12

12. RUMELANGE

US Rumelange lost 9–0 to Dutch team Feyenoord in the first leg of their 1962–3 UEFA Cup match. They hoped to do better in the second leg at their home stadium, but they lost again, this time by a record 12–0.

FEYENOORD ROTTERDAM	VS	UNION SPORTIVE RUMELANGE
9		0
UNION SPORTIVE RUMELANGE	VS	FEYENOORD ROTTERDAM
0		1 2

9

9. STUTTGART

On 22 November 1950, West Germany played their first international game since the end of World War II. The winning goal was scored by Herbert Burdenski, who also wore one of the first ever pairs of football boots with screw-in studs.

11. BASEL

This was the birthplace of Leopold 'Poldi' Kielholz, who played for Switzerland in the 1934 and 1938 World Cups. He was the first Swiss player to score a goal at a World Cup and scored over 100 times for various clubs.

11

SWITZERLAND

BERN ★

EUROPE
ASIA
AFRICA

10. STALDEN

The Ottmar Hitzfeld stadium is home to Swiss side FC Gspon, and can only be reached via cable car. At an altitude of 2,000m, the pitch is made of artificial grass as real grass is hard to maintain on the mountainside.

★ VADU

LIECHTENSTEIN

10

GERMANY, BENELUX AND THE ALPS

Football came to these countries early. The first known game took place in Melle, Belgium, in 1863. Switzerland is now the home of FIFA, while Germany's men's team has won four FIFA World Cups and three UEFA European Championships. The women's team have been Women's World Cup winners twice and European champions eight times.

1. DORTMUND

Borussia Dortmund's Signal Iduna Park has one of the largest single football stands in the world. It holds an incredible 25,000 fans, all wearing their team's home colours, which gives it the nickname the Yellow Wall. The stadium is Germany's largest, holding up to 81,359.

Elbe river

GERMANY

★ BERLIN

Fans of German club FC Union Berlin flock to their club's home ground, Stadion An der Alten Försterei, every Christmas Eve to sing Christmas carols. Approximately 20,000 fans turn up every year.

2. MAGDEBURG

After enduring five games in a row in 2012 without their team scoring once, FC Magdeburg fans decided to help their side out and carried large cardboard arrows into the football ground to point to the goal! It sort of worked, with Magdeburg scoring once, but eventually losing 2–1 to Berliner AK '07.

3. GELSENKIRCHEN

German goalie Manuel Neuer was born here. In 2012, he won half a million Euros for a children's charity when appearing on the German version of the quiz show, *Who Wants to Be a Millionaire?* Neuer is also a movie star, providing the voice of Frank McCay in the German version of the Disney-Pixar movie, *Monsters University.*

5. HERZOGENAURACH

Footballs used in World Cup tournaments have been made here since 1970. The latest designs, such as the Brazuca ball, used at the 2014 World Cup, are tested using a robot leg that kicks each ball 2,000 times or more. The Brazuca ball was also checked out by 600 professional footballers.

4. FRANKFURT

This is the birthplace of German women's striker, Birgit Prinz, who scored an incredible 128 goals for her country between 1994 and 2011, 45 goals more than the second highest scorer, Heidi Mohr.

6. NÖRDLINGEN

Goal machine Gerd Müller started his footballing career at 1861 Nördlingen and scored 51 goals in just 31 league games, before being transferred to Bayern Munich. He would go on to score relentlessly, notching up 735 goals in 793 competitive matches for his club and country.

7. BOBINGEN

Samuel Keplinger refereed a local boys' football match between SSV Bobingen and SV Reinhartshausen in 2008. Nothing unusual in that, except Samuel was just nine years and 302 days old, making him the youngest known football referee.

The Allianz Arena stadium in Munich, Germany, is covered in 2,760 diamond-shaped panels made of plastic. Lights beneath them turn the stadium different colours depending on who is playing there.

Danube river

★ VIENNA

Fans of Rapid Vienna perform a ritual in the last 15 minutes of a match and no one remembers quite how it started. The Rapid Quarter Hour sees them clap their hands fast for the full 15 minutes, to urge their team on.

AUSTRIA

ALPS

8. INNSBRUCK

In 2012, four Austrians — Alexander Kuen, Manuel Larcher and brothers Bernd and Dietmar Neururer — played table football for a marathon 61 hours and 17 minutes. Over 6,000 goals were scored!

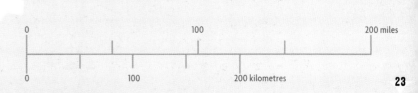

ITALY

Italy is one of Europe's most historic and successful footballing nations. Its top division is called Serie A and contains famous clubs such as Juventus, AC Milan and Inter Milan. Italian clubs have broken the world transfer fee a record 18 times to bring football superstars – from Diego Maradona to Zinedine Zidane – to their teams. The national team, known as the Azzurri for the blue shirts they wear, was the first country to win the FIFA World Cup twice and have won the competition four times overall.

1. CAERANO DI SAN MARCO

The record for most people in the one place playing keepy-uppy (keeping a football in the air) happened in this small town in May 2016. A whopping 1,406 people (about a fifth of the town's population) took part.

2. GENOA

Just one supporter turned up to watch Udinese Calcio in their 2012 Serie A away game against Sampdoria in Genoa. Loyal fan Arrigo Brovedani was first booed by the home fans before later being cheered on, given a football shirt by Sampdoria and invited out for a meal. Brovedani's favourite team won 2–0!

3. TURIN

The biggest table football table was unveiled here in 2015. It measured 121.4m long and had handles for up to 424 players.

When Chilean striker Iván Zamorano joined Inter Milan, he asked for shirt number 9. When he discovered it was already taken by Ronaldo, he instead had 1+8 printed on the back of his shirt!

Po river

4. LA SPEZIA

In 2016, Spezia Calcio versus Bari in Italy's second division, Serie B, was the first game in Italy where footballers could be shown a green card to praise them for friendly or fair behaviour. At the end of the 2016–7 season, the player with the most green cards received an award.

5. SAN MARINO

By 2016, this tiny principality's national team had only won one game in 137 (against Liechtenstein in 2004). In total, the side has let in 591 goals and only scored 21. However, one of their goals was the fastest in international football. Davide Gualtieri scored it in 1993 after just 8.3 seconds of a match against England.

6. FLORENCE

Calcio fiorentino was a type of football game played here over 500 years ago, sometimes on the iced-over Arno river that runs through the city. It was played by nobles and at least three popes. Still played today, the game has 27 players per side, who use both their hands and feet to control the ball.

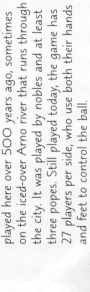

ITALY

7. BARI

The Italian national team unveiled their new kit here in 2016. It was revealed in a street painting of three of the team's players, Gianluigi Buffon, Marco Verratti and Giorgio Chiellini, in the city's main square. The painting was an optical illusion of the players in 3D.

⑦

★ ROME

In 2011, Lazio made an unusual transfer, paying Portuguese club Benfica €125,000. The fee was not for a player, but for a bald eagle called Olimpia that Lazio adopted as a mascot and let fly round its stadium before matches.

VATICAN CITY

⑧

8. NAPLES

After a 0–0 draw in the Euro 1968 semi-final between Italy and the Soviet Union, the German referee, Kurt Tschenscher, tossed a coin to decide which team would progress to the final. Italian captain, Giacinto Facchetti, called correctly and Italy went through.

9. PALERMO

US Palermo are Sicily's most successful team and five times Serie B champions. They play in black and pink, colours suggested in 1905 by Count Giuseppe Airoldi as 'colours of the sad and the sweet'. This reflected the club's results, which were up and down at the time.

⑨

S I C I L Y

One-club man **PAOLO MALDINI** joined **AC MILAN'S** youth system before he became a teenager and only retired in **2009** when he reached the age of **41**. In between, he played more than **900 MATCHES** for the club, winning the **CHAMPIONS LEAGUE** five times and the **ITALIAN LEAGUE** seven times.

AIR AIR AIR AIR

In 1999, Serie A football club Fiorentina began selling an unusual item of football merchandise. Tin cans containing air collected from their Artemio Franchi stadium was sold in three versions, 'Air of the Terraces', 'Dressing Room Atmosphere' and 'Essence of Victory'.

AS Roma signed nine-year-old Belgian footballer, Pietro Tomaselli, in 2014. The club did not watch him at a match or invite him to training. Instead, they viewed his video highlights on YouTube!

S A R D I N I A

After setting a new Italian record in 2016 for not letting in a goal, Juventus keeper Gianluigi Buffon wrote a love letter to the goal he protects during matches, which was published in newspapers and on social media.

EUROPE
ASIA
AFRICA

Former Croatian captain and head coach Slaven Bilić began and finished his playing career with HNK Hajduk Split. In his spare time, Bilić is a guitarist in the Croatian rock band, Rawbau, whose single, *Vatreno Ludilo* ('Fiery Madness') went to number one in Croatia in 2008.

In 2013, tens of thousands of people raced on to the streets of Sarajevo, Bosnia's capital city, to celebrate when the national team qualified for a World Cup for the first time. Vedad Ibisevic scored the crucial winning goal against Lithuania that put Bosnia through.

SLOVENIA
★
LJUBLJANA   ★ ZAGREB

CROATIA

BOSNIA AND HERZEGOVINA

★ SARAJEVO

10. SPLIT

In 2009, Hajduk Split fans made an unusual protest against their club's president, Joško Svaguša, by throwing doughnuts on the pitch before games. Svaguša was the owner of a chain of bakeries in Croatia.

8. STRYMONIKO

This is the birthplace of Angelos Charisteas, who made history at Euro 2004 by scoring the winning goal that gave Greece their first major international title. In total, he scored 25 times for the national side during his career.

7. THESSALONIKI

In 1995, Giorgios (Yórghos) Koúdas was invited to play in one final game for Greece versus Yugoslavia, despite being retired. He became the footballer with the longest international career — 27 years, 319 days. His first game for Greece had been against Australia in 1967!

TIRANA ★

ALBANIA

9. TROGIR

Batarija was the home ground of HNK Trogir until 2009. This scenic ground had a protected historic monument, the tower of St Marco, at one end of the pitch and the complete 15th-century Kamerlengo Castle at the other. Wealthy spectators could book a table at the castle's restaurant and watch the game!

GREECE

ATHENS ★

5. KALAMATA

This is the birthplace of Greek defender Sokratis Papastathopoulos, who started out at AEK Athens and has played 69 games for Greece. His surname is too long to be printed on the back of his football shirt, so he has his first name on it instead.

6. BURSA

Turkish club Bursaspor are known as the 'Green Crocodiles' and have a crocodile as a mascot. They now have a bright green crocodile-shaped stadium roof to match! Opened in 2015, although work on parts of the stadium continued into 2017, the Timsah Arena holds over 40,000 fans.

CRETE

4. SPARTA

The ancient Spartans played a game that historians call Episkyros. It involved 12–14 players on each side, and a lot of teamwork to move the ball up the pitch, while avoiding the other team, and across a line marked at the pitch's end.

MEDITERRANEAN SEA

EASTERN MEDITERRANEAN

This region of the Mediterranean was once dominated by the country of Yugoslavia before it broke into a number of independent nations. Yugoslavian teams finished runners-up at two European Championships and won Olympic football gold in 1960. Clubs from Turkey, Greece, Croatia and Bosnia regularly play in European competitions and, at national level, Greece has won the UEFA European Championship, and both Turkey and Croatia have finished third at a FIFA World Cup.

EUROPE
ASIA
AFRICA

0   100   200 miles

0   100   200 kilometres

1. ISTANBUL

Siyah Çoraplılar ('Black Stockings') was the first Turkish football club featuring solely Turkish players. It was formed in 1901 and disbanded after just one match. The Ottoman Empire, which Turkey was part of, forbade Turks to play the game – so police invaded the pitch and arrested a number of the players!

BLACK SEA

2. ÇORUM

In 2015, Hamit Işık, manager of Turkish third division side, Çorum Belediyespor, was given a stadium ban for arguing with referees. When Işık wanted to watch a crucial promotion play-off game featuring his side, he got round the ban by hiring a crane to lift him above the outer stadium wall to peer in on the game below.

T U R K E Y

★ ANKARA

In 2014, the chairman of Gençlerbirliği, twice winners of the Turkish Cup, banned beards. İlhan Cavcav has been chairman of the club since 1978 and threatened the club's players with fines of 25,000 Turkish lira (£7,000) should any of them should grow one.

Tigres river

In a Champions League match at GSP Stadium, Nicosia, the home of Cypriot club, APOEL, Barcelona set a record for the number of passes made in a single game. The Spanish club attempted 934 passes – more than 10 per minute – and completed 840 of them successfully.

Born in the Croatian city of Osijek, **DAVOR ŠUKER** played for **DINAMO ZAGREB** before moving to **SEVILLA** and, in 1996, **REAL MADRID**. Šuker went on to make **69** appearances for **CROATIA** and was top scorer in the **1998 WORLD CUP**. Šuker's goals helped Croatia to their best ever **WORLD CUP** finish – third – and his **45 GOALS IN TOTAL** remain an all-time record. In 2012, he became **PRESIDENT** of the Croatian Football Federation.

C Y P R U S ★ NICOSIA

3. LIMASSOL

Two brothers in their fifties, Dimos and Renos Christodoulidis, completed 1,013 headers of a football between them without letting the ball drop on 3 October 2013. The pair broke their record the following year with 1,925 headers while standing in the sea off Limassol.

A Mexican wave at a football stadium is when the crowd stands then sits in turn to create the impression of a wave running around the stands. Academics at Eötvös Loránd University in Budapest found that the average speed of a Mexican wave was 12m or about 22 seats per second.

NORTH SEA

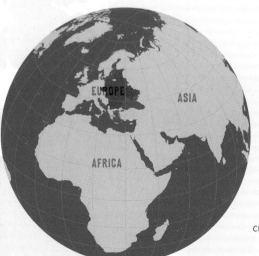

9. MALBORK

This was the birthplace of Grzegorz Lato, the top scorer of the 1974 World Cup, where Poland finished third. He was also an Olympic gold medallist in 1972, when Poland went through the tournament unbeaten.

8. POZNAŃ

Fans of Lech Poznań perform an unusual crowd move, turning their backs to the pitch, putting their arms round their neighbour's shoulders and jumping up and down while chanting. Originally called the Grecque in the 1960s, it is now known as the Poznań.

POLAND

WARSAW ★

2. LUTS

Born in Lutsk, the most-capped Ukrainia footballer Anatoliy Tymoshchuk's luck number is 4. He wears the shirt number 4 or 44 and once tried to buy an apartmen on the 44th floor of a tower block

7. BLŠANY

This was the location of Petr Čech's first professional club, FK Chmel Blšany, before he became famous as a goalkeeper for Chelsea, followed by Arsenal. Čech practises his saves with a pile of water bottles or junk in front of the goal so he can test his reactions when the ball bounces off at odd angles.

Vltava river

⑦ PRAGUE ★

CZECH REPUBLIC

Vistula river

SLOVAKIA

The club badge of Czech team Bohemians 1905 features a kangaroo! The team gave themselves the nickname Bohemians during a tour of Australia in 1927. As they were about to sail home, they were presented with two kangaroos, which were given to Prague Zoo when they reached home.

★ BRATISLAVA

HUNGAR

★ BUDAPEST

⑥

6. SZOMBATHELY

Hungary's most famous goalkeeper, Gábor Király, began and ended his career here with Szombathelyi Haladás. He played more than 100 times for Hungary, and always wore baggy grey tracksuit bottoms instead of shorts.

Amateur Slovakian team TJ Tatran Čierny Balog's ground has a railway track running between the supporters' stand and the pitch. Steam trains run even during matches, when they obscure the game with smoke.

BELGRADE ★

During a 2014 qualifying match for EURO 2016, a drone buzzed the pitch and lowered a banner carrying a political message. This caused uproar, the match was abandoned and both teams were fined €100,000.

SERB

MONTENEGRO

⑤ PRISTINA ★

★ KOSOVO
PODGORICA SKOPJE ★
MACEDONI

5. NIKŠIĆ

Montenegrin club Čelik Nikšić had to travel 1,500km to the Ukraine for their 2012–13 UEFA Europa League match, but did not have the right visas so made a giant detour. Having started the coach trip on Sunday, they did not arrive until Wednesday – a 65-hour journey!

★ TALLINN
E STONIA

L A T V I A
★ RIGA

Belarussian striker Dzimtry Koub celebrated his 2014 headed goal for Trakai against Lithuanian league champions FK Žalgiris in unusual fashion. He raced off the pitch, climbed into the stands and sat in an empty seat so he could applaud himself!

This fascinating collection of footballing countries includes twice World Cup runner-up, Hungary, and Euro 1976 champions, Czechoslovakia (since 1993 the Czech Republic and Slovakia). National teams from this region have won six Olympic football gold medals and, in 2013, Estonia became the first nation to play all the other 52 UEFA countries. The year before, the region held a major international tournament for the first time when Ukraine and Poland co-hosted EURO 2012.

L I THUANIA

VI LNIUS ★

B E L A R U S

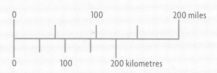

| 0 | | 100 | | 200 miles |
| 0 | | 100 | | 200 kilometres |

★ MINSK
Women's team FC Minsk won every home match they played in the 2013 season, scoring 122 goals in 16 games to win the Belarusian Premier League and adding the Women's Cup to their trophy cabinet.

1. DONETSK
Just before the 2013–4 season started, Shakhtar Donetsk sold three of their best players — Willian, Fernandinho and Henrikh Mkhitaryan — for nearly £100 million. Despite replacing them with lesser-known players, the team won the Ukraine Premier League for the ninth time.

Dnieper river

2

For over ten years, Anatoliy Tymoshchuk wore the same T-shirt under his football shirt before playing games.

★ KIEV
Students at a University in Ukraine's capital city devised a new version of football in 2007. Footdoubleball is played with two different coloured footballs that are in play all the time.

1

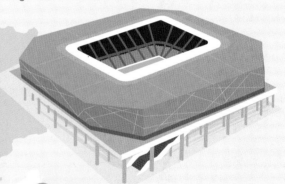

Dniester river

U K R A I N E

4

M O L D O V A

Due to armed conflict in their home city, Shakthar Donetsk has played its home games in the main stadium in Lviv since 2014.

R O M A N I A

CHIŞINÂU ★ **3**

3. TIRASPOL
Tiligul Tiraspol's flight from Moldova, via Budapest and Paris, for a UEFA Cup game ended with them missing a connection and losing most of their luggage. When the team finally arrived in Belgium to play Anderlecht, the Moldovans had to borrow their opponent's away kit, which they were allowed to keep.

4. PITEŞTI
The first professional club of striker Adrian Mutu was here. His pre-match superstitions include stuffing basil leaves in his football socks before putting them on, and wearing his match underpants inside-out.

4

★ BUCHAREST

Danube river

BLACK SEA

B U L G A R I A

Romania's squad for the first ever World Cup in 1930 was selected by Romania's King Carol II instead of the coach Costel Rădulescu. The king travelled with the team to Uruguay on the *SS Conte Verde* and took part in football training with the side on deck.

★ SOFIA
Three generations of the Mihaylov family were goalkeepers who all played for Levski Sofia and won Bulgarian league titles. Biser, Borislav and Nikolay Mihaylov collected a total of nine league titles between them.

THE WORLD CUP

The FIFA World Cup first kicked off in 1930 and has since become football's biggest competition, watched by hundreds of millions of fans on TV and the Internet worldwide. The 2019 Women's World Cup will be held in France and the 2022 World Cup for male teams will take place in the Middle Eastern nation of Qatar. Here are some fun facts about this great competition between the world's leading national football teams.

Brazil have won more World Cup finals games (70 wins and only 17 defeats) than any other nation, and, in 1970, got to keep the Jules Rimet Trophy forever. Sadly, the trophy was stolen from the headquarters of the Brazilian Football Confederation in Rio de Janeiro in 1983 and has never been recovered.

In the 2015 Women's World Cup, 1,353,506 fans witnessed 146 goals scored in 52 matches. Two of those goals were own goals scored by the same Colombian player, Angie Ponce, in the same match, versus Switzerland – a World Cup first.

Belgian referee John Langenus was put in charge of the first ever FIFA World Cup final in 1930. He decided to dress up and refereed the game wearing a dinner suit jacket, knickerbocker trousers and a red striped tie!

After drawing their two qualifying matches, Spain and Turkey played a third match in Rome to decide which team would appear at the 1954 World Cup. After the game ended in a 2–2 draw, a blindfolded 14-year-old Italian boy, Luigi Franco Gemma, picked lots to send Turkey through to the tournament.

When the women's team from Equatorial Guinea reached the 2011 Women's World Cup, they became only the second nation, after Taiwan, where a women's team has reached the tournament but their male counterparts have never qualified. In 2015, Thailand was the third team to achieve this feat.

The 2010 World Cup was the first to be held on the African continent and was a rousing success. A total of 3,178,856 people attended the 64 matches, eating 390,600 hot dogs and drinking more than 750,000 litres of beer!

Scotland travelled to Tallinn in Estonia for their 1966 World Cup qualifying match, only to find their opponents had not turned up. The Scots had to stand through both national anthems, line up and kick off as if starting the game, before the referee blew the whistle for their win after only three seconds.

The FIFA World Cup trophy was introduced in 1974 and is made of 18 carat gold with a malachite base. It stands 36.8cm high and weighs 6.1kg. It is hollow because if it were solid it would weigh 70–80kg and would be too heavy for the winning team to lift!

The original World Cup trophy was stolen from a London exhibition in 1966. It was eventually found in a hedge by a dog called Pickles who became a celebrity, starred in a movie and earned his owner, Dave Corbett, a reward of £6,000.

The fastest ever own goal at a World Cup was unfortunately scored by Bosnia and Herzegovina defender Sead Kolašinac in 2014. Kolašinac scored after just three minutes in a match that saw Argentina win 2–1.

NORTH AND CENTRAL AMERICA

CANADA

ALASKA

SOUTH AMERICA

NORTH AMERICA

BERMUDA

BAHAMAS

TURKS AND
CAICOS ISLANDS

DOMINICAN
REPUBLIC

PUERTO
RICO

HAITI

CUBA

JAMAICA

CAYMAN
ISLANDS

HONDURAS

BELIZE

NICARAGUA

COSTA RICA

PANAMA

GUATEMALA

EL SALVADOR

MEXICO

UNITED STATES

OTHER CARIBBEAN ISLANDS

ANGUILLA

ST MARTIN/
ST MAARTEN

ST BARTHÉLEMY

ANTIGUA AND
BARBUDA

ST KITTS
AND NEVIS

GUADELOUPE

MONTSERRAT

DOMINICA

MARTINIQUE

ST LUCIA

ST VINCENT AND
THE GRENADINES

BARBADOS

GRENADA

TRINIDAD
AND TOBAGO

0   50   100 miles

0   50   100 kilometres

The Oneida Football Club in Boston, USA, was one of the first to be formed outside Europe, in 1862. Now football is played throughout the region. Two of the closest South American nations, Guyana and Suriname, also compete here.

CONCACAF was formed in 1961 to run football here. Its biggest tournament for national teams is the Gold Cup, begun in 1991 and held every two years. The top clubs in the region contest the CONCACAF Champions League each year.

The region hosted the FIFA World Cup in 1970, 1986 and 1994. The US women's team is the world's most successful, winning four of the first six Olympic games and three Women's World Cups in 1991, 1999 and 2015.

0   500   1,000 miles

0   500   1,000 kilometres

EASTERN UNITED STATES

Newark in New Jersey was the location of the first unofficial international football matches between Canada and the USA in 1885. Today, according to FIFA, around 24.5 million men and women, and girls and boys play football regularly throughout the country. The US men's team have won the CONCACAF Gold Cup five times and the women's team have been victors several times in the Olympics and the Women's World Cup.

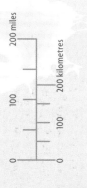

In 1995, Kristine Lilly played her first professional football in America for a club who played in the Continental Indoor Soccer League. That season, she was the only female player in the team! Lilly would go on to become the most capped footballer, male or female, in international football, notching up an astonishing 354 games for the US women's national team.

Born in Rochester, New York State, **ABBY WAMBACH** scored **27 GOALS** in three mini football games at the **AGE OF 5** and has kept on scoring ever since. In 2013, she surpassed Mia Hamm's 158 goals to become the US women's team's **HIGHEST EVER GOAL SCORER**. Wambach retired two years later having scored **184 GOALS IN 255 GAMES** for the national team and winning the **US SOCCER FEMALE ATHLETE OF THE YEAR** six times, more than any other player.

America's Equine Soccer League (AESL) was formed in 2009 to coordinate the growing sport of horse football! Using most of football's regular rules, the game is played on horseback, with the horse or rider's legs and feet moving a giant 101cm-wide inflatable ball.

Each year, an MLS (Major League Soccer) All-Star Game is held that features the best players picked from MLS sides. Until 2005 they were formed into two teams, East and West. In the 2000 match, the East went 3–1 down early in the first half, but roared back to win 9–4 – the highest-scoring all-star game ever.

2. DETROIT

The world's first World Cup match played indoors occurred at the Pontiac Silverdome in 1994 when the US men's team shared a 1–1 draw with Switzerland at the 1994 FIFA World Cup. Four World Cup group games were played on the indoor pitch and it was also used as the home ground for NASL side Detroit Express.

Two Harvard students, Jessica Matthews and Julia Silverman, developed an amazing new football that generates electrical power. The Socket converts the energy generated when the ball is kicked into electricity stored in a battery inside the ball. Playing for 30 minutes can provide three hours of power.

3. BOSTON

The first organised games of football in the USA were played in Boston by the Oneida Football Club, formed by Gerrit Smith Miller in 1862. The team used a football designed by American Charles Goodyear that was made of vulcanised rubber panels glued together.

4. RHODE ISLAND

This is the home of the Fall River Marksmen Football Club. One of their players, Bert Patenaude, travelled to Uruguay in 1930 to take part in the first World Cup, where he scored the first ever hat-trick in a World Cup.

1. CHICAGO

In July 2016, against South Africa, US women's team goalkeeper Hope Solo became the first goalkeeper to keep 100 clean sheets in international football. She has won Olympic gold twice and is a World Cup champion.

MINNESOTA

WISCONSIN

MICHIGAN

Lake Superior

Lake Michigan

Lake Huron

Lake Erie

Lake Ontario

NEW YORK

VERMONT

MAINE

NEW HAMPSHIRE

MASSACHUSETTS

RHODE ISLAND

CONNECTICUT

NEW JERSEY

PENNSYLVANIA

Won by Nov 7th 1863 from

0   100   200 miles
0   100   200 kilometres

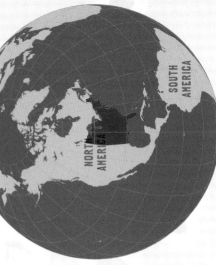

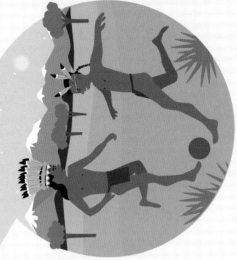

5. NEW YORK CITY

In 2012, American Abraham Munoz climbed up and down 4,698 steps while juggling a football with his feet, head and chest, without letting the football touch the ground. He used steps in Central Park, New York, for this feat.

7. VIRGINIA

In the 1600s, the Powhatan native American peoples played Pasuckuakohowog – 'they gather to play ball with the foot'. The sport could last all day on a pitch as long as 1.6km with 800m-wide goals at each end. According to reports of early settlers to America from Europe, each team could contain hundreds of players!

ATLANTIC OCEAN

WASHINGTON DC

DC United signed America's youngest professional football player in 2004. Freddy Adu was just 14 years old when he came on as a substitute against the San Jose Earthquakes.

6. ST LOUIS

Rick Davis played his club football for the St Louis Steamers indoor football team. In 1984, as captain of the US national team, he scored his country's first goal in an Olympic Games since 1972.

8. ATHENS

The Sanford Stadium hosted the final of the 1996 Olympics' men's football competition. A record 86,117 fans witnessed the first African victory in a major international tournament when Nigeria defeated Argentina 3–2.

9. ORLANDO

In 1996, Orlando's Citrus Bowl Stadium hosted the first ever women's Olympics football match. Tisha Venturini became the US team's first Olympic goal scorer as they beat Denmark 3–0 and went through the tournament unbeaten to win Olympic gold.

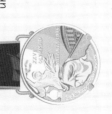

10. MIAMI

The first MLS club of US international Kyle Beckerman was Miami Fusion. He had been a Maryland state wrestling champion before turning to football. Beckerman later played for Colorado Rapids and Real Salt Lake City, and holds the record for the most MLS appearances by an outfield player, playing 412 games by 2017.

GULF OF MEXICO

CARIBBEAN SEA

Missouri river

Ohio river

Mississippi river

Tennessee River

Alabama river

KANSAS

OKLAHOMA

MISSOURI

ILLINOIS

INDIANA

KENTUCKY

TENNESSEE

ARKANSAS

MISSISSIPPI

ALABAMA

LOUISIANA

TEXAS

GEORGIA

SOUTH CAROLINA

NORTH CAROLINA

WEST VIRGINIA

VIRGINIA

MARYLAND

DELAWARE

FLORIDA

Born in Ontario, California, in 1982, **LANDON DONOVAN** played for the **SAN JOSE EARTHQUAKES**, but is best known for his long career with **LA GALAXY**. He is the Galaxy's leading MLS goal scorer with **140 GOALS** and the US national team's leading scorer with **57 GOALS**.

During half-time at the 2013 CONCACAF Gold Cup match between Panama and Mexico, 566 mariachi band musicians performed on the sidelines of the Rose Bowl's pitch with trumpets, violins and guitars to entertain fans and create a world record.

WESTERN UNITED STATES

Many football clubs and thousands of fans live west of the Mississippi river. With over 4,000km between Major League Soccer (MLS) clubs such as the Seattle Sounders and Portland Timbers on the west coast and New England Revolution on the east coast, the MLS is split into two conferences, Eastern and Western. The Western Conference teams have been MLS champions 14 times in the competition's first 20 seasons.

Some of the strangest football shirts were sported by the Colorado Caribous when they played in the North American Soccer League in 1978. Shaped like a horse polo shirt in beige, white and brown with leather tassels running around the chest, the shirt did not inspire the side – they lost 22 of their 30 games.

Lake Superior

WISCONSIN

MINNESOTA

NORTH DAKOTA

SOUTH DAKOTA

Missouri river

NEBRASKA

IOWA

In 2013, Peter Pak-Ngo Pang entered the record books when he refereed a men's league match between Dinamo and Club Lobos in San Jose. He was 80 years and 161 days old, making him the oldest ever referee.

During the 1994 Group B game between Russia and Cameroon at Stanford Stadium, Oleg Salenko became the first player in World Cup history to score five goals in a game. In the same match, Cameroon's 42-year-old striker Roger Milla scored Cameroon's solitary goal to become the oldest goal scorer at a World Cup tournament.

5. SALT LAKE CITY

Nick Rimando joined Real Salt Lake in 2007 and has recorded the most clean sheets (Americans call these shutouts) in the MLS. Rimando has not let in a single goal in 131 of the over 400 MLS games he has played.

MONTANA

WYOMING

BERING SEA

1. ANCHORAGE

In 2006, Carly Butcher became the first Alaskan female footballer to be selected for a US Women's national football team when she made the squad for the United States U17 team.

GULF OF ALASKA

2. MIDDLETON ISLAND

In 2012, a football washed away by a tsunami that struck Japan a year earlier washed up on the shores of this isolated Alaskan island after a journey of over 4,500km. The owner, 16-year-old Misaki Murakami, was traced and the ball returned.

0   100   200 miles
0   100   200 kilometres

3. SEATTLE

Two-time National Women's Soccer League shield winners Seattle Reign hold two NWSL records – the longest run without a win (11 games) in 2013, and in the next season the NWSL's longest unbeaten streak of 16 games.

4. PORTLAND

MLS team the Portland Timbers have an unusual mascot. Timber Joey wields a large chainsaw, slicing off a slab of wood every time the team score a goal. The slice is passed round the crowd and given to the goal scorer at the end of the game.

WASHINGTON

OREGON

Snake river

IDAHO

6. SAN JOSE

Among the merchandise for sale in the San Jose Earthquakes club store are clay heads of striker Steven Lenhart. They hold soil so that fans can plant chia seeds, which grow quickly to form the player's long hair.

7. LAS VEGAS

In 1977, Alan Mayer, goalkeeper for the Las Vegas Quicksilvers, wore a solid plastic crash helmet, a little like those used in ice hockey at the time. The following season, Mayer, then playing for the San Diego Sockers, was voted NASL player of the year.

8. DENVER

The first world championship for table football players was held in Denver in 1975 and won by Steve Simon from Texas. America triumphed each year until 1999, when Belgian Frédéric Collignon won the first of his ten World Championship individual titles.

9. KANSAS CITY

As Sporting Kansas City were beating Colorado Rapids 1-0 in a 2015 MLS game, the stadium's under-pitch sprinkler system turned on and drenched the players. The game was stopped, but players were grateful as temperatures had soared above 35°C.

10. EL SEGUNDO

NASL Soccer was released by Mattel Electronics in 1979 for its Intellivision gaming system. It was the first football computer game that had moving players and some of the rules of the real sport.

Electronic Arts, based in California, publish the world's most popular football computer game series, FIFA. The very first game, FIFA International Soccer, was released in 1993. Twenty years later, FIFA 13 proved a bestseller, with 4.5 million copies sold within the first five days of release.

11. LOS ANGELES

MLS club LA Galaxy experienced Beckham mania when David Beckham signed a five-year deal to play for the team in 2007. The club sold more than 250,000 Beckham football shirts before he had even kicked a ball! Beckham earned around US$1 million per week when he played for them.

12. IRVINE

When the Orange County Blue Stars welcomed new player Jay Göppingen in 2003, the team got a surprise. Göppingen turned out to be a false name, and it was German international striker Jürgen Klinsmann who played for the team for a season just for fun. In 2011, Klinsmann was appointed head coach of the US national team.

13. AUSTIN

Austin Villa, the robot team from the University of Texas at Austin, defeated an Australian team 7–3 in the final to win the 2016 RoboCup Challenge. The humanoid robots, programmed by students, exchange information wirelessly to seek out the goal and predict which of their teammates will reach the ball first.

PACIFIC OCEAN

CALIFORNIA

UTAH

ARIZONA

NEW MEXICO

COLORADO

Colorado River

OKLAHOMA

KANSAS

MISSOURI

ARKANSAS

MISSISSIPPI

LOUISIANA

TEXAS

Rio Grande

GULF OF MEXICO

NORTH AMERICA

SOUTH AMERICA

23 BECKHAM

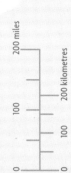

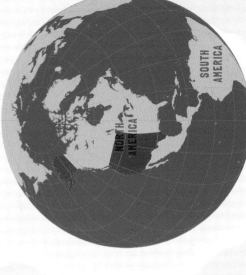

0   100   200 miles

0   100   200 kilometres

CANADA

Although ice hockey and winter sports are the most watched, football is the most popular participation sport here, with over 2.3 million league players. The men's national team have won the CONCACAF Gold Cup twice in 1986 and 2000, and the women's team have won two Olympic bronze medals and finished fourth at the 2003 Women's World Cup.

Brother and sister Lyndon and Charmaine Hooper moved from Guyana to Ottawa when they were aged 11 and 8 respectively. Lyndon played 67 times for Canada. His sister beat him, playing 129 times for the Canadian women's team and scoring 71 goals.

BEAUFORT SEA

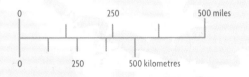

0   250   500 miles

0   250   500 kilometres

1. WHITEHORSE

The 2012 Arctic Winter Games was held here and had indoor football as one of its medal events. The Yukon juvenile women's team reached the final, but lost the game 5–4. The Yukon juniors girls team went one step better, beating Greenland in the final 5–1 to win gold.

Great Bear Lake

Mackenzie river

C   A   N

Great Slave Lake

2. EDMONTON

For two years the Edmonton Drillers played their football indoors at the Northlands Coliseum after their outdoor crowds dropped because of the weather. The team folded in 1982, but new teams competed here in 1996 and 2007.

3. KELOWNA

The Sociology Department at the University of British Columbia at Okanagan offers a course for students about Portuguese football star Cristiano Ronaldo and how he affects society!

PACIFIC OCEAN

4. VANCOUVER

German footballer Holger Osieck became coach of Canada's national men's team in 1998. At the 2000 CONCACAF Gold Cup, he had to call heads or tails as a coin toss to decide whether Canada or South Korea would go through to the quarter-finals. Osieck won and the team went on to win the competition.

6. SASKATOON

Both of Janine Beckie's parents starred for the University of Saskatchewan's basketball teams here, but Beckie turned to football. In 2016, against Australia, she scored the fastest goal ever in Olympic women's football just 20 seconds after kick-off

5. VICTORIA

This is the birthplace of female soccer skills star Chloe Hegland, who appeared on Spanish TV in 2008 and, at the age of ten, set a world record for the most touches of a football while keeping it in the air for 30 seconds. Chloe managed an incredible 163 touches with her feet.

Christine Sinclair scored her first goal for Canada in front of a home crowd during her 29th game for her country at Toronto's Varsity Stadium in a 2–2 draw with the USA. It was her first international match at home. By 2016, she had notched up an incredible 165 goals in 250 matches for her country.

12. BAFFIN ISLAND

The native Inuit peoples played a version of football on snow and ice for centuries. Aqsaqtuk featured a ball made of animal hide stuffed with moss, moose hair and feathers. It was kicked between two sets of lines that acted as the two teams' goals. According to legend, the lines could be up to 16km apart!

BAFFIN BAY

10. ST JOHN'S

In 1985, at the King George V Park Stadium, Canada defeated Honduras 2–1 to qualify for the FIFA World Cup for the first time. One of Canada's goal scorers – George Pakos – had been playing for an amateur team, Vancouver Island Selects, in a park two years earlier when he was spotted at the age of 29.

LABRADOR SEA

11. IQALUIT

An artificial grass pitch was sent here by boat in 2011, one of only three artificial pitches in the whole of Nunavut – an icy territory that makes up about one-fifth of Canada. Teams from other towns often arrive here by boat, snowmobile or even dog sled.

HUDSON BAY

Churchill river

The mascot for the 2015 Women's World Cup was unveiled in Ottawa. Shueme was modelled on a Great White Owl and entertained fans during the tournament's 52 games, the first played solely on artificial grass pitches.

7. TORONTO

MLS club Toronto FC's mascot is not a person in a mascot suit but a real-life bird of prey – a Harris Hawk called Bitchy! It is used to scare away the many seagulls that leave droppings in the stadium and steal food out of supporters' hands.

Great Lakes

9. MONTREAL

In 2015, MLS club Montreal Impact removed eight seats from their stadium to fit in a giant bell bought with donations from supporters. The bell, named North Star, stands over 1.5m tall, weighs more than 700kg and is rung by fans every time their team score a goal.

★ OTTAWA

ATLANTIC OCEAN

The first ever game of the Canadian Championship took place in Montreal in 2008. The championship was won by Montreal Impact.

8. CAMBRIDGE

The local Galt Football Club were chosen to represent Canada at the 1904 Olympics – the first time football had appeared as a competitive medal sport. The team won their two matches to become Olympic champions.

12. MEXICALI

In 2013, at the opening of a new football ground in Mexicali, Baja California's governor Francisco Vega took a penalty kick in front of the press. However, he skewed his shot badly and hit a photographer square in the face!

SONORAN DESERT

Abraham Muñoz ran an entire marathon (42.195km) in 2016 while keeping a football in the air with his feet and head. He only dropped the ball four times in the 5 hours and 41 minutes it took him to complete the distance.

CHIHUAHUAN DESERT

M E X I C O

Rio Grande

11. COMARCA LAGUNERA

Local club Santos Laguna's striker Oribe Peralta scored the fastest goal in Olympic history in the 2012 final of the men's tournament. Peralta struck after just 29 seconds and added a second goal in the 75th minute, as Mexico defeated Brazil 2–1.

SONORAN DESERT

GULF OF CALIFORNIA

10. CULIACÁN

Despite losing two earlier matches 4–0 and 6–0, second division club Dorados de Sinaloa reached the final of Mexico's leading cup competition, Copa MX, in 2012. They won their first major trophy here. The club is nicknamed 'The Big Fish' and has a big fish as both club crest and team mascot.

8. CELAY

Female attacker Maribel Domingue. was signed by a men's professional club, Club Atlético Celaya, in 2004, bu FIFA objected. Instead, Dominguez nicknamed 'Marigol', played 109 time for the women's national team

Mexico has won the CONCACAF Gold Cup a record ten times.

9. DURANGO

This is the birthplace of Mexican goalkeeper Antonio Carbajal Rodríguez who, in 1966, became the first player to appear in five FIFA World Cups (1950–66). Sadly, he retired shortly before Mexico hosted the World Cup for the first time in 1970.

Rio Grande de Santiago

PACIFIC OCEAN

7. GUADALAJARA

Club Deportivo Guadalajara, founded by a Belgian, Edgar Everaert, in 1906, initially featured many Belgian and French players. They adopted a policy of only having Mexican footballers. As a result 'the Goats' have developed homegrown talents such as Javier Hernandez and Omar Bravo.

HUGO SÁNCHEZ wowed fans with his spectacular goals and acrobatic **SOMERSAULTING** celebrations. He played for **UNAM** in Mexico and the **SAN DIEGO SOCKERS** in the USA, before moving to Spain where he won **5 LA LIGA** titles with **REAL MADRID**. In total, he scored **OVER 400 CAREER GOALS**, including **29 GOALS** for Mexico.

In 1987, Mexico had its biggest ever international victory. The team defeated the Bahamas 13–0. Among the goal scorers was Mario Diaz, who came on as a second-half substitute and netted a hat-trick.

6. TOLUCA

At the 1986 World Cup, Paraguay's Cayetano Re became the first coach to be sent off at a World Cup tournament after repeatedly standing on the pitch during a match versus Belgium. At the same World Cup, Uruguay defender José Batista was sent off just 56 seconds after the game started – a World Cup record to this day.

MEXICO

Football has been a passion for Mexicans since the first five-team league was set up in 1902. The Mexican national team have appeared at 15 World Cups and from 1994 onwards have qualified out of their group at the tournament every time. Clubs such as Club América, Cruz Azul and UNAM had together won the CONCACAF Champions League (formerly the Champions Cup) 32 times by 2016.

Cuauhtémoc Blanco invented a new move in the 1990s to get past two or more defenders crowding him. He trapped the ball between his feet, sprang high over the defenders' legs and released the ball in the air, so that when he landed he was ready to run with it, pass or shoot.

1. SAN NICOLÁS DE LA GARZA

All-time leading goal scorer Jared Borgetti scored his last two goals for his country at the Estadio Universitario ground during Mexico's 7–0 defeat of Belize in 2008. Borgetti's 46th and last goal for his country came in the 90th minute.

2. CHICHÉN ITZÁ

A ball game was played several thousand years ago first by the Olmec, then Maya and Aztec civilisations. The players used a solid rubber ball made from latex and the game was played on a large pitch or court made of stone. The Mayan-Toltec city of Chichén Itzá has the largest surviving ball court, which is 146m long and 36m wide.

3. REAL DEL MONTE

GULF OF MEXICO

Mexico's first official football club, Pachua Athletic Club, was formed in 1901 by mineworkers from Cornwall, England. They worked in the Pachua and Real del Monte silver mines and were nicknamed 'the Moles'. A strong connection to Cornwall continues to this day.

The first International Cornish Pasty Festival was held in Real del Monte in 2009, and a museum dedicated to Cornish pasties opened in 2012.

4. VERACRUZ

Veracruz defender Oscar Mascorro takes pre-match superstitions to a whole new level. He always gets out of bed on his right foot first, has a hamburger, apple juice and vanilla milkshake as his pre-match meal, writes M and P in honour of his parents on bandages on his wrists and pulls out a piece of the turf when he walks out onto the pitch!

⑥ ★ MEXICO CITY ④

⑤ **5. ACAPULCO**

This is the birthplace of goalkeeper Jorge Campos. As well as performing spectacular saves and playing for Mexico 130 times, Campos is famous for designing his own very colourful goalkeeping kit and coming out of his goal to join his team's attacks.

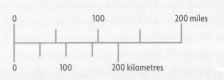

| 0 | | | 100 | | | 200 miles |
| 0 | 100 | 200 kilometres | | |

6. TIKAL

The ancient Mayan city of Tikal has five narrow ball courts with sloping stone walls, in which players played an ancient kicking ball game, Ti Pitziil, with a solid rubber ball. Although usually played for fun, some games were used to settle disputes and the losing team punished with torture or even execution!

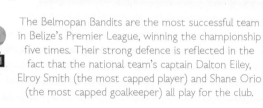

The Belmopan Bandits are the most successful team in Belize's Premier League, winning the championship five times. Their strong defence is reflected in the fact that the national team's captain Dalton Eiley, Elroy Smith (the most capped player) and Shane Orio (the most capped goalkeeper) all play for the club.

6 **BELMOPAN**

BELIZE

5

5. PLACENCIA

In 2011, the two competing top football leagues in Belize merged to form the six-team Belize Premier League, won the first time by Placencia Assassins FC. The Assassins' bloodthirsty pirate skull is one of the most striking club badges in football.

GUATEMALA

HONDURAS

GUATEMALA CITY ★

Until 1992, defenders could pass the ball back to their goalkeeper to pick up. Then the laws of football were changed. The 8,272 spectators, at the El Salvador versus Nicaragua match on 23 July 1992, saw Leonel Cárcamo make the last back pass before the law changed the following day. Cárcamo's side, El Salvador, won the match 5–1.

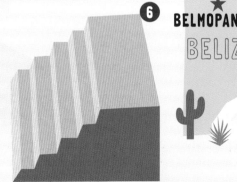

★ **TEGUCIGALPA**

SAN SALVADOR ★ **EL SALVADOR**

N I C A

PACIFIC OCEAN

4. HONDURAS–EL SALVADOR BORDER

Tensions over borders and economics between neighbours Honduras and El Salvador boiled over in 1969 after a three-match series was played to determine who would qualify for the 1970 World Cup. El Salvador won and shortly afterwards invaded Honduras. The 'Football War' lasted just four days, but many people died.

MANAGUA ★

3 Lake Nicaragua

In 2016, Carlos Ruiz scored an incredible five goals during Guatemala's 9–3 win over St Vincent and the Grenadines. This made *El Pescadito* – 'the Little Fish' as he is nicknamed – the world's leading goal scorer in World Cup qualifying with 39 goals in total. His first game for Guatemala was in 1998.

2. PUNTARENAS

In 2011, Joel Campbell was playing his club football at Puntarenas Fútbol Club SAD, on loan from CD Saprissa, when he was transferred to an English club Arsenal. He has since spent five seasons on loan, each season with a different club in Spain, Greece or Portugal. He has also played more than 50 times for Costa Rica since 2011 and, in 2016, scored twice in the country's stunning 4–0 win over the USA when qualifying for the 2018 World Cup.

While playing for **EURO KICKERS** in Panama's Asociación Nacional Pro Fútbol (ANAPROF), **JOSÉ ARDINES** was the **LEAGUE'S TOP SCORER** in six seasons in a row. His record ended in 1996, but in 1997 he set another record, yet to be beaten in Panama, **SCORING 11 GOALS** in a 13–2 victory over Ejecutivo Jrs.

Estadio Cuscatlán in the city of San Salvador is the largest football ground in Central America. It can hold up to 53,400 spectators and is used regularly by El Salvador's national team as well as league clubs Alianza FC and CD Atlético Marte. It has also been used for a world record bid for the most people brushing their teeth at one time – 13,380 people in 2005.

In 1921, four of the seven nations that make up Central America played their first ever international games in Guatemala City as part of the Independence Centenary Games. Costa Rica won the tournament ahead of Guatemala, El Salvador and Honduras, and remain the strongest footballing nation in the area. Football tends to be less popular than baseball in Nicaragua and Panama, while Belize only played its first international, versus El Salvador, in 1995.

Club Deportivo Olimpia was founded in Honduras in 1912 as a baseball team, but became the country's most successful football club. Known as the Whites or the Lions, the club's teams have won 30 league championships as well as the CONCACAF Champions Cup twice, in 1972 and 1988.

In 2016, the president of Nicaragua, Daniel Ortega awarded his country's highest medal, the Order of Augusto Cesar Sandino, not to a war hero but to a footballer and one from another country – Diego Maradona from Argentina.

3. DIRIAMBA

Diriangén FC are one of the oldest clubs in Central America, having formed in 1917. They are also Nicaragua's most successful side with 25 Primera División titles, over ten more than their fiercest rival, Real Esteli. Diriangén's women's team have won the country's women's football championship four times since it began in 1996.

G U A

CARIBBEAN SEA

NORTH AMERICA

SOUTH AMERICA

CD Saprissa were named after Ricardo Saprissa Aymá, the man who bought the team their first set of football shirts in 1935. Two years later, they switched to purple. From the 1980s, their noisy fans, all dressed in purple, gave the club their nickname of *El Monstruo Morado* – 'the purple monster'. The club's mascot is a purple dragon.

C O S T A   R I C A

②

 ★ SAN JOSE

Panama Canal   P A N A M A

①

 ★ PANAMA CITY

1. PÉREZ ZELEDÓN

This is the birthplace of Keylor Navas, who in 2016 became the first Costa Rican to win the UEFA Champions League. Navas began his career at CD Saprissa before moving to Spain and being bought by Real Madrid for more than €10 million. Costa Rica's first choice goalkeeper, Navas, set a record by not letting in a single goal in his first eight Champions League games for Real Madrid.

Panama have twice reached the final of the CONCACAF Gold Cup, in 2005 and 2013, and on both occasions were defeated narrowly by the USA. In the 2015 Gold Cup, Panama defeated the US team to finish third in the competition. In all three competitions, Jaime Penedo was in goal and was voted goalkeeper of the tournament in 2003 and 2013, but lost out to the USA's Brad Guzan in 2015.

★ **NASSAU**

B A H A M A S

ATLANTIC OCEAN

★ HAVANA

In February 2016, Jhoen Lefont Rodriguez plunged into the pool at the Hotel Meliá Cohiba, Havana, and broke his own world record for the most headers of a football while treading water. Rodriguez managed to head the ball 1,513 times.

6. GRAND'ANSE

Many Caribbean footballers move to Europe or North America to play football. Sony Norde, who was born in Grand'Anse, went to Asia instead. He was named India's I–League player of the season twice and also the Bangladesh Premier League's most valuable player in 2014.

TURKS AN CAICOS ISLANDS

C U B A

8. CAYMAN ISLANDS

In 2007, Alyssa Chin made her debut for the Cayman Islands women's national team versus Puerto Rico, just seven days after celebrating her 13th birthday!

C A Y M A N
I S L A N D S

THE ISLAND OF HISPANIOLA (DIVIDED INTO HAITI AND THE DOMINICAN REPUBLIC)

H A I T I

7. MONTEGO BAY

This is the birthplace of Theodore Whitmore, who scored both goals in Jamaica's one victory at a World Cup finals, when the 'Reggae Boyz' defeated Japan 2–1 in 1998. Whitmore scored 24 goals in total and has since had four spells as caretaker or permanent manager of the Jamaican national team.

J A M A I C A

7

6

PORT-AU-PRINCE

KINGSTON

When the Jamaican team qualified for the 1998 World Cup, a giant inflatable football approximately 15.5m in diameter was constructed, and its panels filled with good luck messages from fans. The ball was displayed in Jamaica, New York, London and finally, Paris, where World Cup matches were held.

Born in Canaan on the island of Tobago, **DWIGHT YORKE** played in a 1989 pre-season friendly versus Aston Villa who were on tour. He impressed **VILLA** manager Graham Taylor so much that he was signed by the English club and later moved to **MANCHESTER UNITED**, where he won the **CHAMPIONS LEAGUE** and **THREE PREMIER LEAGUE TITLES**. He played more than **70 TIMES** for Trinidad and Tobago and captained the **SOCA WARRIORS**, as they were nicknamed, at the **2006 FIFA WORLD CUP**.

Joseph Gaetjens won the Haitian National Championship with Etoile Haitienne in 1942 and 1944 before moving to the United States to study accountancy. To make ends meet, he worked as a dishwasher in a restaurant. Picked for the US national team, he appeared at the 1950 World Cup and scored the only goal in the US team's surprising win over a strong England side.

5. PUERTO RICO

Puerto Rico had to wait 30 years and 40 matches before they achieved their first win in international football. El Huracán Azul ('the Blue Hurricane'), as the team is nicknamed, achieved their historic win with a 3–0 victory over the Bahamas at the 1970 Central American and Caribbean Games.

CARIBBEAN

Football is hugely popular among the thousands of islands that make up the Caribbean region but, with mostly small populations, the teams here struggle to make an impact worldwide. Cuba were the first Caribbean nation to reach the FIFA World Cup in 1938. Fighting for places against big CONCACAF teams, such as Mexico and the USA, has meant that only three have made it since: Haiti in 1974, Jamaica in 1998 and Trinidad and Tobago in 2006.

4. BRITISH VIRGIN ISLANDS

André Villas-Boas managed the British Virgin Islands national team in 2000 and 2001. He was just 21 when he was appointed. Ten years later, he became Chelsea's head coach after they paid Porto a record £13.3 million.

In 2015, the national team of St Kitts and Nevis, a small nation with a population of under 60,000, played their first ever matches in Europe. The 'Sugar Boyz' triumphed over Andorra to record the first win by a Caribbean Football Union team on a European opponent's home turf.

2. ANTIGUA AND BARBUDA

Legendary West Indian cricketer Viv Richards also played football for the Antigua and Barbuda national team during qualifying for the 1974 FIFA World Cup. The team did not get through, but Richards was able to win a World Cup in cricket twice, in 1975 and 1979.

3. VIRGIN ISLANDS

These islands have no national stadium for their team to play in. Instead, when they had home matches to try to qualify for the 2014 World Cup, they used Lionel Roberts Park, a baseball stadium. They had to buy in and fit a layer of grass over the dirt of the baseball diamond.

1. PORT OF SPAIN

In a 1989 World Cup game at the National Stadium, US defensive midfielder Paul Caligiuri scored the goal that propelled the US national team to a FIFA World Cup for the first time in 40 years. The goal became known in America as the 'shot that was heard around the world'.

Map labels

DOMINICAN REPUBLIC
★ SANTO DOMINGO

SAN JUAN ⑤ ★
PUERTO RICO

BRITISH VIRGIN ISLANDS ④

VIRGIN ISLANDS ③

ST MARTIN / ST MAARTEN   ANGUILLA
ST BARTHÉLEMY
ST KITTS AND NEVIS ★
BASSETERRE
② ANTIGUA AND BARBUDA
★ ST JOHN'S

MONTSERRAT

GUADELOUPE

DOMINICA
ROSEAU ★

MARTINIQUE
FORT-DE-FRANCE ★

ST LUCIA ★
CASTRIES

ST VINCENT AND THE GRENADINES
KINGSTOWN ★

BARBADOS
BRIDGETOWN ★

GRENADA
★ ST GEORGE'S

CARIBBEAN SEA

TRINIDAD AND TOBAGO
PORT OF SPAIN ★ ①

NORTH AMERICA

SOUTH AMERICA

0   100   200 miles

0   100   200 kilometres

SOUTH AMERICA

FRENCH GUIANA

SURINAME

GUYANA

VENEZUELA

COLOMBIA

BRAZIL

PERU

ECUADOR

NORTH AMERICA

SOUTH AMERICA

ANTARCTICA

SOUTH ATLANTIC OCEAN

SOUTH PACIFIC OCEAN

PARAGUAY

URUGUAY

CHILE

ARGENTINA

FALKLAND ISLANDS
Part of the UK

For a continent with just ten footballing member nations, South America punches well above its weight in global football. It hosted the first World Cup tournament and produced the first world champions. South American sides have won nine of the 20 World Cups held so far, and have also been runners-up five times.

Football in South America is run by CONMEBOL, which was formed in 1910. The Copa America began in 1916 and remains the oldest surviving continental competition – it is 44 years older than the UEFA European Championships.

The game was brought to South America in the 1860s by European sailors, traders and railway workers. Today, South America exports many of its most talented players to play abroad, including Argentina's Lionel Messi to Spain and Chile's Alexi Sanchez to England. More than 1,700 Brazilians play professional football in other countries.

0   500   1,000 miles

0   500   1,000 kilometres

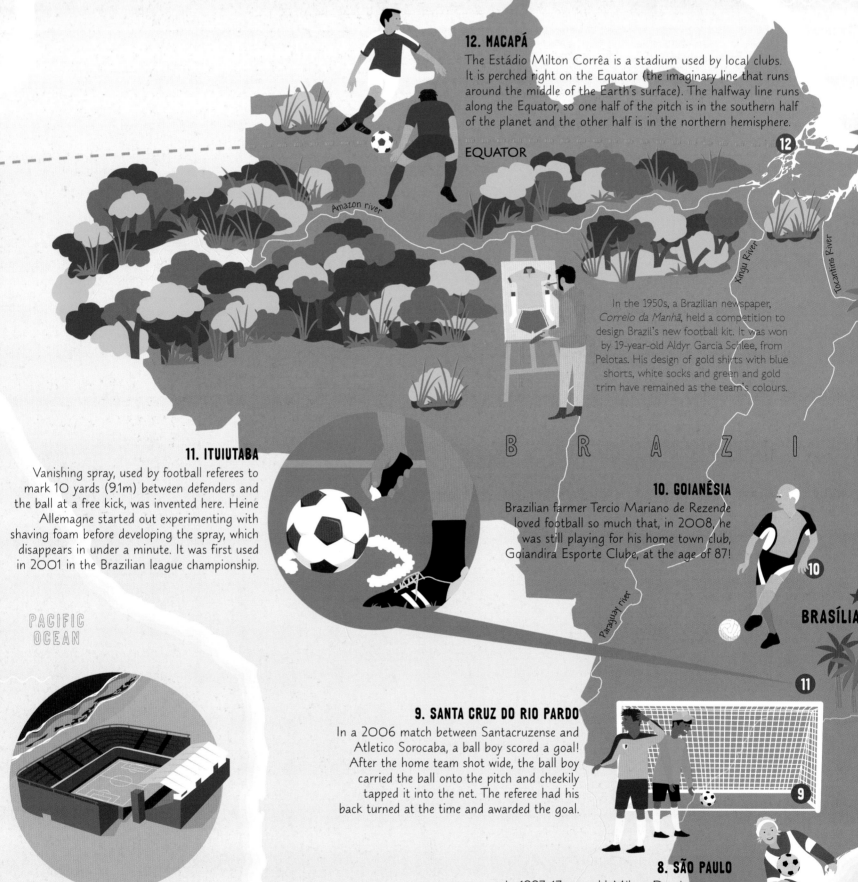

12. MACAPÁ

The Estádio Milton Corrêa is a stadium used by local clubs. It is perched right on the Equator (the imaginary line that runs around the middle of the Earth's surface). The halfway line runs along the Equator, so one half of the pitch is in the southern half of the planet and the other half is in the northern hemisphere.

EQUATOR

Amazon river

In the 1950s, a Brazilian newspaper, *Correio da Manhã*, held a competition to design Brazil's new football kit. It was won by 19-year-old Aldyr Garcia Schlee, from Pelotas. His design of gold shirts with blue shorts, white socks and green and gold trim have remained as the team's colours.

B R A Z I L

Xingu River

Tocantins River

11. ITUIUTABA

Vanishing spray, used by football referees to mark 10 yards (9.1m) between defenders and the ball at a free kick, was invented here. Heine Allemagne started out experimenting with shaving foam before developing the spray, which disappears in under a minute. It was first used in 2001 in the Brazilian league championship.

10. GOIANÊSIA

Brazilian farmer Tercio Mariano de Rezende loved football so much that, in 2008, he was still playing for his home town club, Goiandira Esporte Clube, at the age of 87!

BRASÍLIA

Paraguay river

PACIFIC OCEAN

9. SANTA CRUZ DO RIO PARDO

In a 2006 match between Santacruzense and Atletico Sorocaba, a ball boy scored a goal! After the home team shot wide, the ball boy carried the ball onto the pitch and cheekily tapped it into the net. The referee had his back turned at the time and awarded the goal.

8. SÃO PAULO

In 1997, 17-year-old Milene Dominguez set a world record for keeping a football in the air with touches of her feet, legs and head for 9 hours, 6 minutes with an incredible 55,187 touches. Five years later she became the most expensive female footballer when she was transferred to Spanish side Atlético Madrid.

The first Beach Soccer World Championships kicked off on Copacabana Beach in Rio in 1995. Beach soccer is a five-a-side game with footballers playing in bare feet. Brazil thrashed the Netherlands 16–2, England 13–2 and the USA 8–1 in the final to become champions.

7. PORTO ALEGRE

Ronaldinho played 97 matches for Brazil, but first became famous when he was 13 years old. When he played for a local team in Porto Alegre that won a game 23–0, Ronaldinho scored all 23 goals!

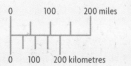

0   100   200 miles

0   100   200 kilometres

Anyone who calls their nation 'o País do Futebol' ('the Country of Football') must be football crazy! That is certainly the case with Brazil. Top clubs such as Corinthians, Santos and Flamengo, and their star players Pelé, Zico, Ronaldo, Marta and Neymar have lit up the game. The Brazilian national team are the only side to appear in every single FIFA World Cup and have won the competition five times — more than any other team.

1. NATAL

In 2015, at the city's Arena das Dunas Stadium, Marta Vieira da Silva became the first Brazilian footballer to score 100 goals for her country when she scored twice in Brazil's 6–0 win over Mexico. She is also the only female footballer to win FIFA's World Player of the Year award five times (2006–10).

EQUATOR

HI
MY NAME IS

Zinedine Yazid Zidane
Thierry Henry Barthez
Eric Felipe Silva Santos

Marta developed her football skills at an early age playing street games in her neighbourhood.

2. MACEIÓ

After enjoying two years living in France, a Brazilian goalkeeper from Maceió, Petrucio Santos, named his son after many of the France's 2006 World Cup team. The boy was named Zinedine Yazid Zidane Thierry Henry Barthez Eric Felipe Silva Santos!

Goalkeeper Rogério Ceni's career began in 1993 and finished when he retired in 2015. In that time, he made more than 1,200 appearances and scored an incredible 131 goals as a free-kick and penalty taker – the most by any top-level goalkeeper.

3. SALVADOR

In 2012, the Vitoria Football Club removed the four red horizontal stripes from their traditional home football shirts. They promised to add the red back if its fans donated blood to medical centres. Blood donor numbers rose sharply and the club duly added a red stripe back each time they played.

EDSON ARANTES DO NASCIMENTO, better known as **PELÉ**, is considered one of the finest footballers of all time. This great Brazilian attacker scored **OVER 1,200 GOALS** for his club, **SANTOS**, and a further **77 GOALS** for **BRAZIL** with whom he won **3 WORLD CUPS**, the first in 1958 when he was just 17 years old. He scored **93 HAT-TRICKS** and, on 31 occasions, scored **4 GOALS** in a single game.

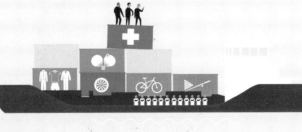

4. SANTO ANDRÉ

Germany had an entire base called Campo Bahia built especially for the 2014 World Cup in Brazil. It had 14 villas, 65 rooms, a swimming pool, spa and full-sized football pitch. The German team shipped out over 20 tonnes of kit for the team, including mountain bikes and table-tennis tables. It must have helped as the Germans won the tournament.

5. BELO HORIZONTE

During a tense 1998 derby game between local rivals Atletico Mineiro and América Futebol Clube, Edmilson Ferreira celebrated a goal after scoring in the 20th minute for Mineiro. He ran over to the fans of the opposing team, nicknamed 'the Rabbits', pulled out a carrot hidden in his football shorts and ate it.

Paraná river

ATLANTIC OCEAN

6. RIO DE JANEIRO

In 2014, in the Morro de Mineira *favela* – a deprived area of Brazil's capital city – the world's first electricity-generating football pitch was installed. The pitch has 200 tiles underneath artificial turf, which turn the movement of players stepping on them into electricity that, in turn, powers the pitch's six LED floodlights.

200 miles
0   100   200
0   100   200 kilometres

PACIFIC OCEAN

1. ARICA

The Carlos Dittborn Stadium saw Chile reach the semi-final of the World Cup for the first time in 1962 after beating the Soviet Union 2–1. The Chileans consumed the traditional food or drinks of their opponents before each of their matches. They ate cheese before defeating Switzerland, spaghetti before beating Italy and drank vodka before this victory over the Russians.

2. TOCOPILLA

Tocopilla-born Alexis Sanchez played for Chilean club Colo Colo before starring in Europe for Barcelona and Arsenal. He is the first attacker to play 100 times for Chile.

3. COPIAPÓ

A landslide trapped 33 Chilean miners 676m below ground in the Atacama desert for 69 days in 2010. A television cable was sent down a small hole, so the miners could watch footage of the Chilean national team playing a match versus Ukraine. One of them, Franklin Lobos, had been a professional footballer, so he provided a match commentary for the others.

4. SANTA LUCÍA

In a 2009/10 cup match between Juventud Alianza and General Paz Juniors, the teams contested one of the longest ever penalty shootouts in South America. It took 42 penalties to decide the winner – Juventud.

5. VIÑA DEL MAR

During the 1962 FIFA World Cup quarter-final match between England and Brazil, a small black dog invaded the pitch and started chasing the ball. Eventually, England striker Jimmy Greaves caught him.

The dog was adopted by one of Greaves' Brazilian opponents, the winger Garrincha, who named the dog Bi.

6. CÓRDOBA

A small museum devoted to footballs was founded here by Roberto A. Fuglini. By 2005, he had collected a world record

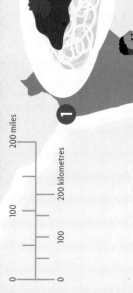

CHILE

SANTIAGO ★

ANDES

ARGENTINA

PARAGUAY

Paraguay river

Paraná river

Salado river

ASUNCIÓN

In 1989, goalkeeper José Luis Chilavert held his nerve to score the winning goal for Paraguay in the last minute of a World Cup qualifier. In total, Chilavert scored 67 goals for his country and clubs. While playing for Argentinean club Vélez Sarsfield in 1999, he became the first goalkeeper to score a hat-trick in the same game.

Uruguay only had a population of approximately 1.7 million in 1930, but the country still won the FIFA World Cup, a feat it repeated in 1950. This was the first nation to win the Copa América 15 times.

URUGUAY

7. ROSARIO

In 1998, the Maradonian Church was set up by fans of Diego Maradona, one of Argentina's finest footballers. The 'church' followers celebrate Christmas on Maradona's birthday (30 October) and adopt Diego as their middle name!

LA MANO DE DIOS

MONTEVIDEO ★

BUENOS AIRES ★

Most professional football in Uruguay is based in and around the capital city of Montevideo. Clubs from this city have won all of the first 113 league championships.

After their fierce rivals, Peñarol, unveiled a 309m-long flag, Nacional fans decided to beat them at their own game! In 2013, they unfurled a 600 x 50m flag in their stadium, the Estadio Centenario in Montevideo, Uruguay.

SOUTHERN SOUTH AMERICA

Football was brought to these four South American nations by sailors or immigrants from Europe in the late 19th century. All four countries have won the highly prized Copa América, although Chile had the longest wait. They made their debut in 1916 and first won it 99 years later!

Born in Rosario, Argentina, **LIONEL MESSI** was such an exciting **YOUNG TALENT** that Barcelona coach Carles Rexach hurriedly signed him as a **12-YEAR-OLD**, writing the contract on a paper napkin. Messi proved to be a **SENSATIONAL** signing. He has already scored over **500 GOALS** for **BARCELONA** and, in 2012, **91 GOALS** in total for **ARGENTINA** and **BARCELONA** — a record for a single year.

9. MAR DEL PLATA

When France turned up here for a 1978 World Cup match against Hungary, they discovered their shirts were the same colour as their opponents – white. They had to borrow a set of green-and-white striped shirts from local team Club Atlético Kimberley.

Negro river

Argentina's blind football team reached the final of the first World Blind Soccer Championships in 1995 and won the competition in both 2002 and 2006. Players play with a ball full of ball bearings that make a jangling sound as it moves, so the visually impaired footballers can hear it.

ATLANTIC OCEAN

An Argentinian club was among the first to consider implanting microchips with season ticket details in the arms of their fans — Club Atlético Tigre ran a trial in 2016. The idea is that the fans never have to worry about leaving their ticket at home!

STANLEY ★
FALKLAND ISLANDS

8. TALCAHUANO

In 1914, fans at the El Morro stadium here saw what is thought to be football's first ever bicycle kick, performed by 20-year-old Chilean forward Ramón Unzaga Asla.

Famous Argentinean footballer and manager, Diego Simeone, was sent off at the age of 11, when he was a ball boy for Vélez Sarsfield. In the 1982 match, he threw an extra ball onto the pitch to try to help his team launch an attack.

CHILE

ANDES

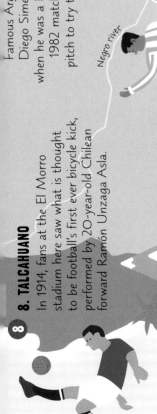

PACIFIC OCEAN

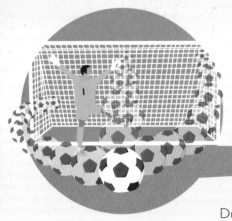

8. PELILEO

In a 2016 Ecuadorian third division league game, Pelileo Sporting Club delighted their fans with a record thrashing of rival club, Indi Native. Pelileo defeated their opponents 44–1, with winger Ronny Medina scoring an amazing 18 goals.

QUITO ★

E C U A D O R

In 2014, Vanessa Arauz became head coach of Ecuador's Women's National football team aged 25. She led the team in the 2015 Women's World Cup, where she became the youngest ever World Cup coach, male or female.

Marañón river

PACIFIC OCEAN

7. GUAYAQUIL

During a 2016 match in Ecuador's top league, the Primera A, between River Plate and Aucas, a swarm of bees flew on to the pitch and terrorised the players so much that the referee had to abandon the game. It was replayed two days later.

The much-travelled Peruvian attacker Nolberto Solano is so famous that his face has appeared on postage stamps. And when he and his fiancée Claudia got married, the whole wedding was broadcast live on national TV in Peru.

6. SECHURA

In 2014, local club La Bocana were leading 4–1 in a Copa Perú game when five members of the opposing team, Defensor Bolivar, fell down at the same time, pretending they were injured. The referee stopped the game, but only after La Bocana had scored again, knocking Bolivar out of the competition.

GALÁPAGOS ISLANDS (PART OF ECUADOR)

PACIFIC OCEAN

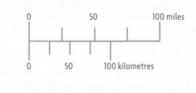

```
0          50         100 miles
0      50       100 kilometres
```

P E R U

5. GALÁPAGOS ISLANDS

Denise Andrea Pesantes was born on Santa Cruz island and in 2015 became the first player from the Galápagos Islands to play in a World Cup when she was selected for Ecuador's women's team. As a child, Pesantes used to play in bare feet with a football covered in plasters to hide its rips and holes.

LIMA ★

A popular way of declaring your support for your favourite football club in Peru's capital city is to dress pet dogs in the colours of the football team!

Born in Puente Piedra, **PERU'S** most famous footballer, midfielder **TEÓFILO CUBILLAS**, began playing for local club **ALLIANZ LIMA** when he was only 16 years old. He scored **5 GOALS** in the **1970 WORLD CUP**, and in 1978 became the **FIRST FOOTBALLER** in the world to score **5 OR MORE GOALS** in **2 WORLD CUPS**.

Universidad San Martin only began playing in 2002 and do not own a football stadium, however they won Peru's league championship, the Primera Division, in 2007, 2008 and 2010. The club was formed by the university's dentistry students and their mascot at matches is a giant tooth!

4. MOUNT SAJAMA

In 2001, a game of football was played on the snow-covered top of South America's second highest mountain. Two teams, one made up of international guides and mountaineers, and the other of local Bolivians, first climbed the 6,542m mountain then laid out a 50 x 35m pitch on which they played two 20-minute halves using orange-coloured footballs.

PACIFIC OCEAN

Striker Monica Quinteros made her debut for the Ecuador national women's team at the age of 13. Quinteros helped Ecuador qualify for their very first Women's World Cup in 2015.

All three nations joined FIFA in the 1920s, and both Peru and Bolivia have won the Copa América, the leading competition for national teams in South America. Ecuador turned down an invitation to appear at the first World Cup in 1930 and did not reach the competition until 2002. Six years later, LDU Quito became the champion club of South America, winning the continent's premier club competition, the Copa Libertadores, the first time a club from Ecuador has triumphed.

1. CERRO DE PASCO

This mining town in the Andes is home to the world's highest football stadium. The Estadio Daniel Alcides Carrión is located at an altitude of 4,380m and is home to Unión Minas who, in 2016, played in the Peruvian third division.

AMAZON RAINFOREST

NORTH AMERICA

SOUTH AMERICA

ANTARCTICA

When Bolivia's new national team coach Angel Guillermo Hoyos was appointed in 2016, he named a squad of 93 players (7 goalkeepers, 27 defenders, 34 midfielders and 25 strikers) to pick from, instead of the usual 20 or 24.

ANDES

2. WARNES

In 2014, the football-mad President of Bolivia, Evo Morales, signed to play as a midfielder for Sport Boys Warnes. The club played in the top division of the Bolivian leagues – the Liga de Fútbol Profesional Boliviano.

Lake Titicaca

★ LA PAZ

Perched at an altitude of 3,637m above sea level, Bolivia's national stadium, the Estadio Hernando Siles, is one of the highest in the world. In 2009, it was home to Bolivia's most stunning international victory – a 6–1 win over mighty Argentina. Joaquin Botero scored a hat-trick.

❷
❸

★ SUCRE

3. SANTA CRUZ DE LA SIERRA

This is the birthplace of Víctor Hugo Antelo, the all-time leading goal scorer in the Bolivian league, with a whopping 350 goals. Despite his goal-scoring prowess and 28-year footballing career, Antelo was only picked to play for Bolivia 11 times.

❹

B O L I V I A

0   100   200 miles

0   100   200 kilometres

JAPAN

In 2016, East Fukuoka High School's football team scored using an unusual free kick routine. Two sets of three of the team's own players formed a wall in front of the defensive wall set up by their opponents and ducked as the free kick was taken, confusing the opposition.

AUSTRALIA

In 2007, Ellyse Perry played her first matches for the Australian women's national teams in both football and cricket! Perry became the first player, male or female, to appear at both a cricket (2009) and football (2011) World Cup.

SPAIN

In a 2013 UEFA Champions League game against Paris Saint-Germain, Barcelona midfielder Xavi Hernández made more passes than any other player on the pitch – 96 out of 96 attempts – a 100% success rate.

45
HALF

TURKEY

When Galatasary and Fenerbahçe, two of Turkey's leading clubs, play each other, sparks often fly. In April 1996, Fenerbahçe lost at home to their rivals and to add insult to injury, Galatasaray manager Graeme Souness ran onto the pitch and planted a Galatasaray flag in the centre circle.

THE NETHERLANDS

Ajax are the Netherlands' most successful football club. They have won the top Dutch league, the Eredivisie, a record 33 times, and the European Cup/UEFA Champions League four times.

TUVALU

With space at a premium on Polynesian islands, there is only one full-sized football pitch on Tuvalu. All matches in the Tuvalu A-Division are played there and all the clubs are based on nearby Funafuti.

COLOMBIA

Passionate Colombia supporter Gustavo Llanos attends every national team game dressed up as a bright orange, blue and red giant condor bird, the country's national symbol. He is sometimes suspended from ropes by the fans so that he can hang down from the stadium!

00 TIME

EQUATORIAL GUINEA

At the 2015 African Cup of Nations, Ghana's goalkeeper Brimah Razak brought his favourite Spiderman action figure onto the pitch and laid it down next to his goal for luck. Unfortunately, Ghana were beaten by the Ivory Coast.

GERMANY

In autoball, teams of two cars per side nudge a giant 1.2m-diameter football around the pitch. This game was first played on the pitch of Karlsruhe club FC Frankonia in 1933.

AZERBAIJAN

In 2012, Vugar Huseynzade was appointed as a consultant to Azerbaijan club FC Baku and a year later was made coach of their A team. His only football experience was playing the computer game, Football Manager!

BRAZIL

The first ever floodlit football match in Brazil was played in 1923 on a pitch lit up by tram headlights. AA Republica beat SE Linhas e Cabos 2–1.

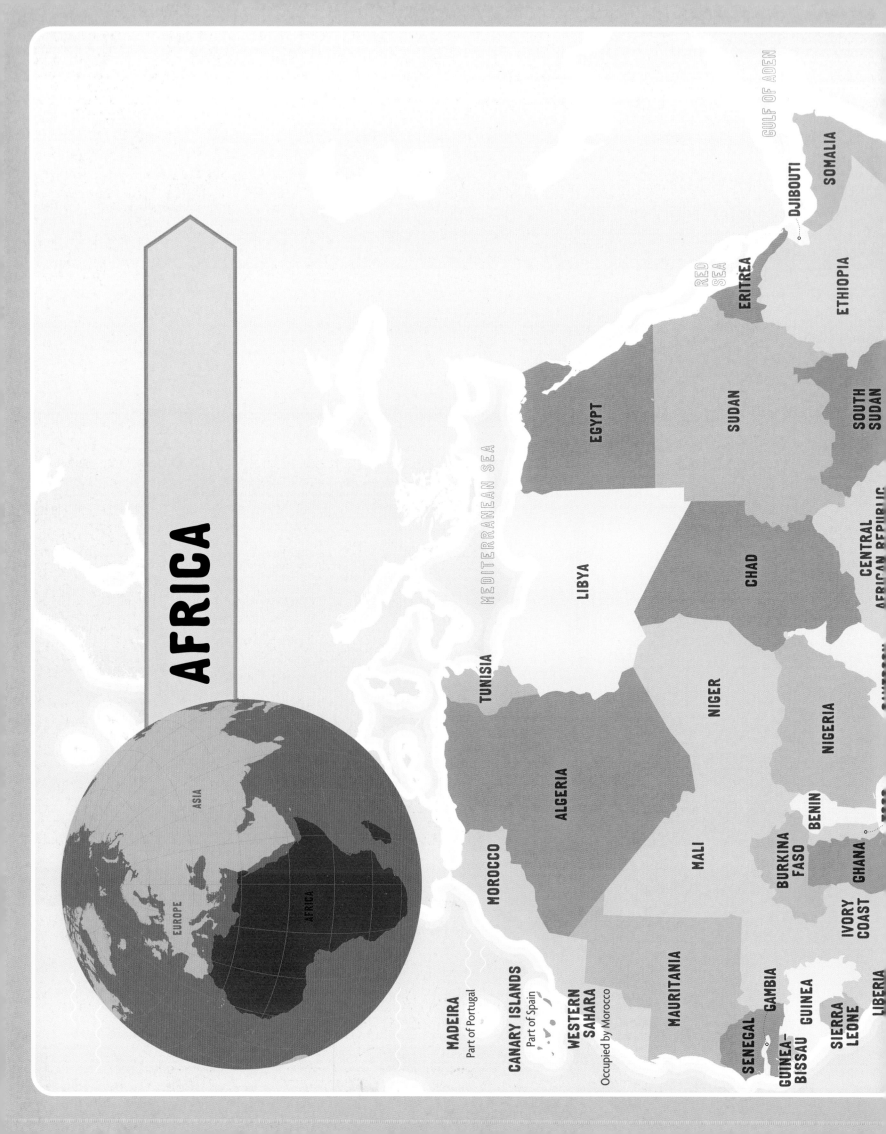

AFRICA

ASIA

EUROPE

AFRICA

MADEIRA
Part of Portugal

CANARY ISLANDS
Part of Spain

WESTERN SAHARA
Occupied by Morocco

MOROCCO

TUNISIA

MEDITERRANEAN SEA

ALGERIA

LIBYA

EGYPT

RED SEA

GULF OF ADEN

DJIBOUTI

SOMALIA

ERITREA

ETHIOPIA

SUDAN

SOUTH SUDAN

CHAD

CENTRAL AFRICAN REPUBLIC

MAURITANIA

MALI

NIGER

NIGERIA

SENEGAL

GAMBIA

GUINEA-BISSAU

GUINEA

BURKINA FASO

BENIN

SIERRA LEONE

IVORY COAST

GHANA

LIBERIA

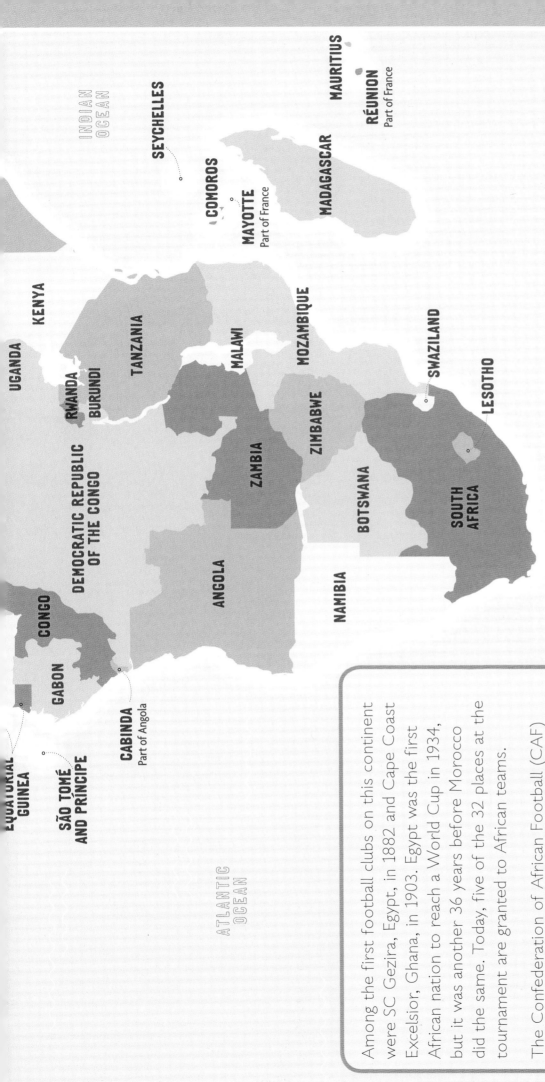

INDIAN OCEAN

SEYCHELLES

COMOROS

MAYOTTE
Part of France

MADAGASCAR

MAURITIUS

RÉUNION
Part of France

UGANDA

KENYA

RWANDA
BURUNDI

TANZANIA

MALAWI

MOZAMBIQUE

SWAZILAND

LESOTHO

ZIMBABWE

ZAMBIA

BOTSWANA

SOUTH AFRICA

DEMOCRATIC REPUBLIC OF THE CONGO

ANGOLA

NAMIBIA

CONGO

GABON

EQUATORIAL GUINEA

SÃO TOMÉ AND PRÍNCIPE

CABINDA
Part of Angola

ATLANTIC OCEAN

Among the first football clubs on this continent were SC Gezira, Egypt, in 1882 and Cape Coast Excelsior, Ghana, in 1903. Egypt was the first African nation to reach a World Cup in 1934, but it was another 36 years before Morocco did the same. Today, five of the 32 places at the tournament are granted to African teams.

The Confederation of African Football (CAF) was formed in Sudan in 1957 and runs the sport on the continent. It boasts 56 member countries and organises the African Cup of Nations for men and women. Nigeria have dominated the women's competition, winning 9 of the first 11 tournaments. The Nigerian men's team became the first African nation to win the Olympic football gold in 1996, followed by Cameroon in 2000.

500 miles

0   250   500 kilometres

0   250   500 kilometres

ATLANTIC OCEAN

Saving a penalty in a 2010 Moroccan cup game, versus Maghreb Fez, goalkeeper Khalid Askri turned to face the crowd and celebrate. He should have kept his eye on the ball, which spun backwards and crept over the goal line!

RABAT ★
2

ATLAS MOUNTAINS

MOROCCO

2. CASABLANCA

This was the birthplace of Noureddine Naybet, who won three Botola (Moroccan league) championships with Wyad Casablanca and has played a record 115 times for Morocco. The national team are known as the Atlas Lions, after the Atlas mountains that run through part of the country.

ALGIERS

3

In 1990, 105,032 fans squeezed into the Stade 5 Juillet 1962 (named after the date of Algeria's independence from France) to witness the home side win their first ever African Cup of Nations competition. Chérif Oudjani scored the only goal to defeat Nigeria.

A L G E R I A

WESTERN SAHARA
(OCCUPIED BY MOROCCO)

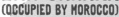

M A U R I T A N I A

3. MASCARA

Lakhdar Belloumi joined his local club GC Mascara at the age of 19 and was playing for the Algerian national team by 1978, less than a year later. The African Footballer of the Year in 1981, he scored the winning goal in Algeria's 2–1 defeat of West Germany in 1982, one of the World Cup's biggest ever shocks. He later managed GC Mascara and the Algerian beach football team.

NOUAKCHOTT
★

1. NOUADHIBOU

During the Mauritanian Super Cup in 2015, FC Tevragh-Zeina and ACS Ksar were drawing 1–1 when the referee stopped the game in the 63rd minute and made both teams play a penalty shootout! Was the country's president (who was at the match) bored with how the game was going?

In 2013, Algerian freestyle footballer Abdellah Belabbas appeared on a Turkish TV show and set a world record for the most touches of a football – 219 – hanging from a lamppost.

1

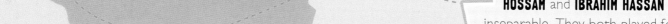

NORTHERN AFRICA

Football reached Africa from Europe at the end of the 19th century and is now the most popular sport in all of the North African nations. Sandy or rocky deserts cover large areas of these countries, so stadiums are mostly concentrated in a small number of cities and large towns. North African national teams have appeared in the final of the African Cup of Nations on 19 occasions.

Born in Cairo, Egyptian twins **HOSSAM** and **IBRAHIM HASSAN** appeared inseparable. They both played for **AL-AHLY** in Cairo, then **PAOK SALONIKA** in Greece, followed by **NEUCHÂTEL XAMAX** in Switzerland, before returning to Egypt and playing for Al-Ahly again as well as rival team **ZAMALEK**. Defender Ibrahim played **125 MATCHES** for Egypt, while striker Hossam is Egypt's leading goal scorer, with **69 GOALS** in **169 GAMES**. Both have won **14 EGYPTIAN PREMIER LEAGUE TITLES**.

4. RADÈS

Nicknamed 'the blood and golds' for their unusual playing colours, Espérance Sportive de Tunis have won the Tunisian league a record 26 times, including seven times in a row from 1998 to 2004. In 2011, they won their second African Champions League crown.

TUNIS

In 2015, Sarah Samir, from Sharqia in northeast Egypt, became the first female referee in the country to take charge of a men's national league game when she refereed Wadi Degla FC versus Tala'ea El-Gaish SC in Cairo.

TUNISIA

MEDITERRANEAN SEA

★ TRIPOLI

6. ALEXANDRIA

The first ever Arab Women's Championship was held in Alexandria in 2006. Seven teams contested the competition with Algeria defeating Morocco in the final 1–0. The biggest scoreline in the competition was Tunisia thrashing Syria 10–0.

90:00	
TUNISIA	10
SYRIA	0

5. BENGHAZI

In 2000, fans of Al Ahly Benghazi released a donkey on the pitch wearing the shirt of the rival team, Al Ahli Tripoli. The latter's captain was the son of Libya's ruler, Colonel Gaddafi so, soon after, Al Ahly Benghazi's training ground was demolished by bulldozers and the team relegated from the Libyan Premier League.

7. PORT SAID

Born in Port Said and playing for local club Al-Masry SC, Abdulrahman Fawzi in 1934 became the first African to score at a World Cup. He scored two goals against Hungary in a 4–2 defeat.

★ CAIRO

RED SEA

LIBYA EGYPT

Nile river

Al-Ittihad is Libya's most successful club, winning the Libyan Premier League 16 times, including six times in a row (2005–10). The team, who play their games at the Tripoli Stadium, were, in 2007, the first team from Libya to reach the semi-final stage of the African Champions League.

Egyptian Sahar El-Hawari was not allowed to play football because she was a girl. However, she scoured Egypt for potential players, trained them at her parents' villa in the early 1990s and was delighted to see an Egyptian women's national team qualify for the 1998 Women's African Cup of Nations. In 2000, she helped set up the first women's league.

SUDAN

SAHARA DESERT
BOUNDARY

Appearing at the Gezira Youth Club in Cairo in 2012, Amr Abdel-Fadeel managed to keep a football in the air without it touching the ground for one hour, making a world record 8,230 touches of the ball during this time.

KHARTOUM ★

North Khartoum-born Hytham Mostafa Karar was captain when Sudan qualified for the 2008 African Cup of Nations. He has also played the most times for Sudan, making 103 appearances between 2000 and 2012.

Sudan hosted the first African Cup of Nations in 1957 and finished either second or third in three out of the first four tournaments. They hosted the competition again in 1970, the first to be televised live, and defeated Ghana in the final to be crowned champions. After an appearance in 1976, they did not qualify again for 32 years.

EUROPE   ASIA

AFRICA

0	250	500 miles

0	250	500 kilometres

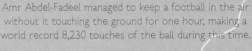

EASTERN AFRICA

Despite many conflicts and natural disasters in this region, including disease and famine, football is enjoyed by millions. Most of the countries are members of CECAFA – the regional football organisation that runs competitions such as the CECAFA Cup for national teams and the Kagame Interclub Cup, which has been won six times by Tanzanian club Simba SC.

0   100   200 miles

0   100   200 kilometres

1. WAU

Al Salaam Wau FC became South Sudan's first league champions in 2011, after an epic quarter-final match versus Etihad climaxed in a long penalty shootout that Al Salaam won 16–15. The team are owned by the country's police force and most of their players are either policemen or students.

Kampala Capital City Authority Football Club (KCCA FC) really celebrated becoming champions of the 16-team Uganda Premier League in 2016. The team conducted three days of trophy parades on the back of trucks around different districts of Kampala, where they were greeted by thousands of fans.

Uele river

SOUTH SUDAN

JUBA ★

South Sudan became an independent nation in 2011 and the following year its national football team played their first full international game at Juba, drawing 2–2 with Uganda.

CONGO

DEMOCRATIC REPUBLIC OF THE CONGO

UGANDA

Many football fans in parts of East Africa have no electricity supply to power a TV, and batteries for radios are too expensive. Rwandan company Nuru Energy, based in Kigali, has built pedal-powered electricity generators for isolated homes.

Congo built a spanking new stadium, the Stade Municipal de Kintélé, for the 2015 All-Africa Games. Ghana's women's national team won their first ever All-Africa Games gold medal in the 60,000-capacity ground.

KAMPALA ★

Lake Victoria

★ **KIGALI**

RWANDA

★ **BUJUMBURA**

Congo river

BURUNDI

Lake Tanganyika

BRAZZAVILLE ★ **KINSHASA**

2. BENA TSHADI

In 1998, tragedy struck at a local football game between Bena Tshadi and visiting side, Basanga. A fierce lightning blast left 11 players dead and around 30 injured.

CABINDA
Part of Angola

TANZANI

3. LUBUMBASHI

Tout Puissant Mazembe have won the Linafoot – the top league in the Democratic Republic of the Congo – a record 15 times. The club's nickname is 'Les Corbeaux' ('the Ravens'), although the team's logo is a crocodile with a ball in its mouth.

ATLANTIC OCEAN

Mobutu Sese Seko, president of Zaire (after 1997, Zaire became DR Congo), changed the name of the national football team from 'the Lions' to 'the Leopards' so that the nickname matched the leopardskin hat that he always wore. When the team qualified for the 1974 World Cup, he gave each player a house and a green Volkswagen car.

Lake Nyasa

ERITREA
ASMARA ★

Red Sea FC are Eritrea's most successful club side, winning the country's top league 12 out of 21 times since it was first held in 1994.

RED SEA

After pelting the pitch with bottles and plastic vuvuzelas during a 2013 African Cup of Nations match versus Zambia, Ethiopian fans said sorry at their next game versus Nigeria. They unveiled a giant banner saying, 'We apologise for our behaviour, but we love the game.'

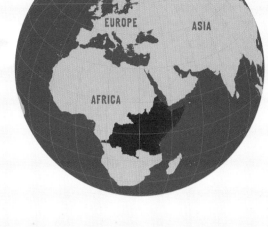

DJIBOUTI

GULF OF ADEN

★ DJIBOUTI

Football is Djibouti's most popular sport, despite the national team's poor performance — by the end of 2016 they had only won two out of 71 international games.

ETHIOPIA

Blue Nile river

★ ADDIS ABABA

Ethiopia took part in the first African Cup of Nations in 1957, and in 1962, in Addis Ababa, won the competition for the first and only time. Two of the team's four goals were scored by Mengistu Worku despite suffering a black eye when the opposition goalkeeper missed the ball with his punch and caught Worku's face.

SOMALIA

Somalia's first football league for children between the ages of 8 and 14 kicked off in 2016. FIFA donations of football kits, shin pads, boots and balls for 200 players enabled the 12 youth teams to enjoy competitive football for the first time.

Jubba river

5. NAKURU

Since 1980, superfan Isaac Juma Onyango has not missed a single home match. The father of 11 is famous for decorating his body and dancing at matches. In 2010, he was given a lifetime achievement award by Kenya's football association.

★ MOGADISHU

INDIAN OCEAN

MOUNT KENYA Tana river

KENYA

★
NAIROBI

MOUNT KILIMANJARO

A Marabou stork interrupted a crucial World Cup qualifying game in Nairobi in 2005. The stork strutted across the pitch of the Nyayo National Stadium during Kenya's 0—0 draw with Morocco.

Nairobi-born Mcdonald Mariga Wanyama became the first footballer from Kenya to play in the UEFA Champions League when he played for Italian club Inter Milan in 2010. His brother, Victor, plays for Tottenham Hotspur in England and their father, Noah, played for AFC Leopards, Kenya's most successful club.

DODOMA

④
4. DAR ES SALAAM

Young Africans are the most successful team in Tanzania with 21 league titles compared to their fierce local rivals in Dar es Salaam, Simba SC, who have 18. When the teams met in 2008 and Young Africans won 1—0, delighted club officials gave the team's players all the ticket money from the more than 60,000 fans.

The 2015 African Beach Soccer Championship, held in the Seychelles, saw a surprise winner when Madagascar defeated three times champions Senegal in the final. The tournament's most valuable player was also from Madagascar, and has one of football's longer names – Tokinianaina Randriamampandry!

1. LUANSHYA

This was the birthplace of Zambia's greatest ever player, Godfrey Chitalu. He made his debut for Zambian club Kabwe Warriors in January 1972. By the end of 1972, Chitalu had built up an astonishing 107 goals for his club and country. For the Zambian national team, he scored 79 goals in 111 games.

LUANDA ★

Never say a match is over. At the 2010 African Cup of Nations, Angola seemed to be cruising at 4–0 against Mali with just 11 minutes to go and a passionate 45,000 home crowd urging them on. Then it all went wrong. Mali scored four times, the last coming from Mustapha Yatabaré in injury time, so the match ended in a 4–4 draw.

3. VICTORIA FALLS

Tragedy struck the Midlands Portland Cement football team in 2008 when their coach ordered them to swim in the Zambezi river before a match. One of their players never returned, believed drowned or eaten by the crocodiles that inhabit the waters.

★ LUSAKA

Luando river

HARARE ★

4. TSUMEB

In the 2004–5 NFK Cup game between KK Palace and Civics at Tsumeb, the game ended in a 2–2 draw and went straight to a penalty shootout. This lasted a long, long time as a record 48 penalties were taken, 15 of which were saved or missed, before KK Palace went through 17–16.

BOTSWANA

Limpopo river

WINDHOEK ★

At the 2014 African Cup of Nations match in Windhoek's Independence Stadium, South Africa's Portia Modise scored twice against Algeria. In doing so, she became the first African footballer, male or female, to score a century of goals for her country.

In 2010, Botswana recorded a rare victory in qualifying over the more highly rated Togo team. Weirdly, as Togo began the long bus journey back to their home country, a fake team pretending to be Togo were in action, playing Bahrain in the Middle East.

GABORONE ★

NAMIBIA

★ PRETORIA (TSHWANE)

ATLANTIC OCEAN

MBABANE ★ **★ MAPUT**

SWAZILAND

SOUTH AFRICA

The vuvuzela horn is blown at many matches in South Africa. The world's biggest working vuvuzela was built by Hyundai South Africa and placed next to a road to celebrate the 2010 World Cup. It was 35m long, 5.5m in diameter at its widest point, and blown by air compressors!

Orange river

BLOEMFONTEIN ★

★ MASERU

LESOTHO

Cape Town jeweller Yair Shimansky celebrated the 2010 World Cup held in South Africa by creating the world's most expensive football. The ball is covered in 6,620 white diamonds and 2,640 black diamonds, weighs over 2kg and is valued at around £2 million.

In the 1970s, Alfred Baloyi invented the Makarapa. He took a hard miner's hat and decorated it with football badges, scenes, signs and horns. Often worn with giant glasses, this popular headwear is seen at South African football matches. One football fan, Sadaam Maake, has a collection of over 200 different designs!

LOVE & PEACE

★ CAPE TOWN

2. BLANTYRE

The most successful club in Malawi are the Big Bullets, also known as the People's Team. They perform an amazing victory dance when they win the Malawi Premier Division, which they have done 13 times. They also contest a local derby in Blantyre with rivals, Mighty Wanderers, and both clubs share the 50,000-capacity Kamuzu Stadium.

★ **LILONGWE**

Lake Nyasa

MALAWI

②

mbezi river

MOZAMBIQUE

5. BULAWAYO

Zimbabwe's most famous footballer and goalkeeper, Bruce Grobbelaar, began his career with Bulawayo-based Highlanders and won the Chibuku Cup. Highlanders have won nine Zimbabwe Premier Soccer League titles, while Grobbelaar went on to play in Canada before being transferred to Liverpool in 1981.

. NKOWANKOWA

n 2005, Beka Ntsanwisi formed a local ootball team of local grandmothers, some of vhom were in their 80s. The aim was to use ootball to improve health. The team were called Vakhegula Vakhegula — meaning 'Grannies, Grannies' in the local Xitsonga language.

Football was brought to this part of Africa by European settlers, military forces and missionaries. The region's strongest teams, for example in South Africa, compete regularly in the African Cup of Nations. All the nations are members of COSAFA, which organises competitions such as the COSAFA Cup and COSAFA Women's Championship for national teams from the region.

COMOROS ISLANDS

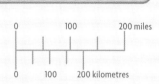

The most astonishing scoreline ever in world football occurred during the 2002 Madagascan championship, known at the time as the THB Champions League. Defending champions SO l'Emyrne were so upset at refereeing decisions in a previous match that they started scoring own goals. By the time the referee blew his whistle for full time, the score was 149–0.

★ **ANTANANARIVO**

MADAGASCAR

RÉUNION ISLAND   ⑥   MAURITIUS

6. RÉUNION

Réunion football club, Jeunesse Sportive Saint-Pierroise, made a surprise signing in 2016 — the former France, Liverpool, Marseille and Lazio striker Djibril Cissé. The club has won the island's top league 16 times, the first occasion back in 1956.

Ferroviáro Maputo were hugely embarrassed when their celebrations got out of hand in 2015. While the players celebrated their last-minute goal, which they thought gave them victory, their opponents, K-Stars from Zambia, got back into position, restarted the game and scored a long-range equaliser into an open goalmouth.

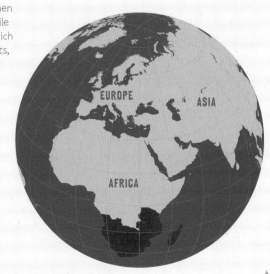

INDIAN OCEAN

8. JOHANNESBURG

In 2013, at the FNB Stadium in Johannesburg, 52-year-old Stephen Keshi became the youngest person to win the African Cup of Nations as both player and coach. The FNB Stadium, with its multi-coloured, tiled outer surface looking like an African cooking pot, is the biggest in Africa with a capacity of 94,736.

WESTERN AFRICA

This region is a real powerhouse for footballing talent. Its national and club teams are highly successful in African competitions, and hundreds of the region's talented players, including Serge Aurier, Seydou Keita and Yaya Toure, play their club football in Europe.

Southampton manager Graeme Souness signed Ali Dia, from Dakar, convinced that he was the cousin of FIFA World Player of the Year, George Weah. It was, in fact, one of Dia's friends pretending to be George Weah on the telephone. Dia arrived on a short-term contract, but was soon substituted when it became obvious that he was not a top footballer!

2. SIKASSO

Mali hosted the African Cup of Nation in 2002 and Cameroon unveiled their new strip with armless football vests instead of shirts. FIFA banned them from wearing the vest tops at the 2002 Wor Cup, so the team sewed on black sleeves

CAPE VERDE
1
ISLANDS

ATLANTIC OCEAN

DAKAR ★

S E N E G A L

★ BANJUL

G A M B I A

★ BISSAU

GUINEA-BISSAU

G U I N E A

Senegal river

BAMAKO ★

Niger river

BURKINA FASO

★ OUAGADOU

CONAKRY ★

SIERRA LEONE

FREETOWN ★

I V O R Y C O A S T

G H A N A

1. CAPE VERDE ISLANDS

In 2000, this country's national team, known as the 'Blue Sharks', were ranked 182nd in the world. This all changed in 2013, with the provision of 25 grass pitches, better coaching and the team's first appearance at the African Cup of Nations. In March 2016, after beating sides that included Portugal, they were ranked 31st in the world, the highest-ranked of all the African nations.

LIBERIA

YAMOUSSOUKRO ★

MONROVIA ★

3

4 ★ LOI
ACCRA

4. CAPE COAS

Ghana reached the final of the African Cup of Nation for a record fourth time in a row in 1970 and ha their flamboyant goalkeeper Robert Mensah partly t thank. Mensah, wearing his oversized cap, pulled off string of saves in the earlier rounds. In some matches if opponents were not on the attack, he pulled ou a newspaper and started reading it while in goa

GEORGE WEAH

played for two clubs in Monrovia, Liberia — **MIGHTY BARROLLE** and **INVINCIBLE ELEVEN** — before moving to Europe where he played for **MONACO, AC MILAN** and **PARIS ST GERMAIN** among others. In 1995, he became the **FIRST AFRICAN FOOTBALLER** to be awarded **FIFA WORLD PLAYER OF THE YEAR**. He used some of his earnings to fund the **LIBERIAN NATIONAL TEAM**, once hiring a private jet for the team when their scheduled flight to Ghana for a match was cancelled.

GULF OF GUINEA

3. ZWEDRU

This was the birthplace of attacker Collins John. He began his professional football career in the Netherlands with FC Twente in 2002 after they paid local side DES Nijverdal an unusual transfer fee — a set of encyclopedias! Two years later, John moved on for a more usual fee — £600,000 to English team, Fulham.

Home advantage really counted for something in the Nigeria Premier League in 2013. Gombe United won 18 of their 19 matches at home that season, drawing the other game. However, 'the Desert Scorpions' lost all 19 away games. Another team, Kaduna United, also lost all of their away games and won 17 out of 19 of their other games at home.

8. KANO

One of the world's greatest unbeaten runs ended in 2015 when Nasarawa United defeated Kano Pillars FC at the Sani Abacha Stadium 2–1, with Nasarawa's first goal coming from a former Pillars' player, Manir Ubale. This marked the 12 years and 202 home league games in a row since Kano Pillars had last tasted defeat!

Five of the 12 clubs in the Chad Premier League, including Gazelle FC and Foullah Edifice FC, play their games at the same stadium, which is named after a Chad high jump athlete! The Stade Idriss Mahamat Ouya in N'Djamena holds 20,000 people and has an artificial grass pitch. Since 2004, all the league champions have played their home games at this ground.

N I G E R

★ NIAMEY

Niger river

C H A D

★ N'DJAMENA

Logone river

Idriss Kameni was just 16 years old when he was put in goal for Cameroon at the 2000 Olympic Games. He proved unflappable and almost unbeatable as he pulled off save after save, which resulted in Cameroon defeating Brazil, Chile and Spain in the final to win the tournament, making Kameni the youngest Olympic football gold medallist.

ENIN

N I G E R I A

★ ABUJA

6. ASABA

Ifeyani Chiejine became the youngest player at a Women's World Cup when she played against Denmark in the 1999 tournament, aged just 16 years, 1 month. The 1.63m attacker, nicknamed 'Smally', played for Nigerian clubs Flying Babes FC, Queens of Abuja and Pelican Stars while still in her teens.

ORTO-NOVO

★ ⑤

⑥

⑧

C E N T R A L
A F R I C A N
R E P U B L I C

All of the nine clubs that were victors in 40 seasons of the Central African Republic League up to 2016 have been based in the country's capital city, Bangui. AS Tempête Mocaf are the leading side with 12 league titles.

BANGUI ★

MALABO ★

★ YAOUNDÉ

C A M E R O O N

E Q U A T O R I A L
G U I N E A

⑦

G A B O N

★ LIBREVILLE

Ogooué river

Cameroonian Rigobert Song has played in 34 consecutive African Cup of Nations games. It is just one of many records that he holds, including the most appearances at African Cup of Nations tournaments (8), most matches played for Cameroon (137) and one unwanted record: the first player to be sent off at two World Cups (2002, 2006).

LAGOS

n 2013, the world's largest football shirt was unveiled in Teslim Balogun Stadium nd took up almost all of the pitch. The hirt measured 73.55m wide from sleeve o sleeve and was a whopping 89.67m long.

7. BITAM

This is the birthplace of Pierre François Aubameyang, who played more than 80 matches for Gabon. His son, Pierre-Emerick Aubameyang, is the national team's leading goal scorer and was voted Africa's best player in 2016. A lover of superheroes, Aubameyang Jr sometimes celebrates by pulling out a Batman or Spiderman mask from his sock and wearing it!

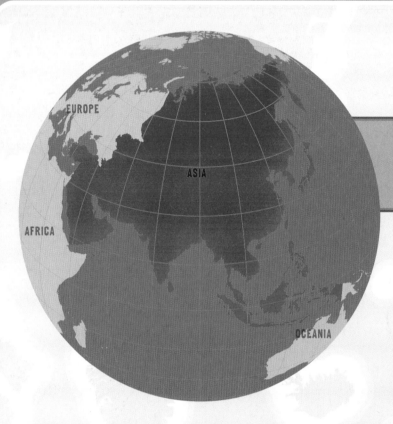

EUROPE

AFRICA

ASIA

OCEANIA

ASIA

RUSSIA
Sits in both
Europe and Asia

TURKEY
Sits in both
Europe and Asia

GEORGIA

ARMENIA

UZBEKIST

AZERBAIJAN

TURKMENIS

LEBANON

ISRAEL

SYRIA

IRAQ

IRAN

JORDAN

KUWAIT

BAHRAIN

QATAR

SAUDI
ARABIA

UAE

OMAN

YEMEN

Parts of the world's most populous continent began playing football in the 19th century. India's first club, Mohun Bagan AC, was formed in Kolkata in 1889 and, 16 years earlier, naval cadets in Japan were taught the game by British sailors in Tokyo. Two thousand years before this, versions of ball-kicking games were played in China, Korea and Japan.

Major football competitions are today run by the Asian Football Confederation (AFC), which has its headquarters in Malaysia. It administers the Asian Cup for national teams, as well as the Asian Champions League for top clubs. More than 20 clubs have won this competition, including teams from Iran, Israel, China, Japan and Qatar.

In 2006, Asia welcomed Australia into the AFC and the Australian men's national team, the Socceroos, have performed well, finishing runners-up in the 2011 Asian Cup and hosting and winning the 2015 competition.

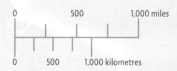

0   500   1,000 miles

0   500   1,000 kilometres

ARCTIC OCEAN

RUSSIA

BERING SEA

ZAKHSTAN

MONGOLIA

KYRGYZSTAN

NORTH
KOREA

TAJIKISTAN

SOUTH
KOREA

JAPAN

GHANISTAN

CHINA

KISTAN

NEPAL
BHUTAN

PACIFIC OCEAN

MYANMAR
(BURMA)

INDIA

TAIWAN

LAOS

BANGLADESH

THAILAND

VIETNAM

PHILIPPINES

SRI
LANKA

CAMBODIA

MALAYSIA

BRUNEI

SINGAPORE

INDONESIA

INDIAN OCEAN

EAST TIMOR

NORTHERN ASIA

Russia spans the whole of northern Asia and stretches into eastern Europe. It was part of the Soviet Union between 1922 and 1991, when its leading football clubs played in the Soviet Top League. They now compete in the Russian Premier League. On the international stage, the Soviet Union were the first European champions, winning EURO 1960. They have since been runners-up three times (1964, 1972, 1988). In 2010, the country was announced as FIFA World Cup hosts in 2018.

ARCTIC OCEAN

2. ST PETERSBURG

Three-time Russian Premier League winner Andrey Arshavin studied fashion at the St Petersburg State University of Technology and Design. He has designed ranges of women's clothing and several of his fashion creations are on display in the university's museum.

1. KALININGRAD

To see 2018 World Cup matches held in the Arena Baltika stadium, Kaliningrad, spectators from Russia have to travel through either Belarus or Latvia, as well as Lithuania, to reach them! Kaliningrad is more than 1,200km from Moscow.

MOSCOW ★

In 2014, 32 Bayern Munich fans could not get tickets for a UEFA Champions League game against CSKA Moscow. Instead, they rented the 18th floor of an office building that overlooked the ground!

3. VORONEZH

This was the home of FC Energy Voronezh, Elena Danilova's club when she became the youngest ever goal scorer at a Women's World Cup in 2003. At the age of just 16, she scored against the eventual champions, Germany.

Volga river

R U S S

Ob

5. SAMARA

Russia's first-ever public museum of football opened in Samara in 2007. The museum houses memorabilia donated by local fans, including the camera that took photos of the first football match in Samara in 1911.

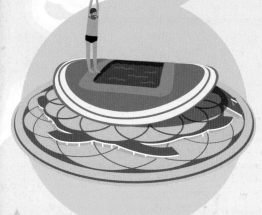

4. KAZAN

The stadium of two-time winners of the Russian Premier League, FC Rubin Kazan, was filled with water in 2015 when the ground hosted the World Aquatics Championships. The Kazan Arena also hosts 2018 World Cup matches and boasts the largest TV screen (4,030m^2) in Europe.

Oleg Veretennikov is the leading goal scorer in the Russian Premier League with 143 goals. He played for ten different Russian clubs and was the league's top scorer in three seasons, yet only played four times for the Russian national team.

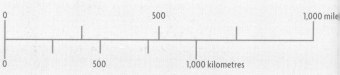

0   500   1,000 miles

0   500   1,000 kilometres

In 2014, the logo for the 2018 World Cup was unveiled by Russian cosmonauts on board the International Space Station orbiting 400km above Earth. The live event was broadcast via Russian television.

In 2006, Luzhniki Stadium's home club, Spartak Moscow, got stuck in a traffic jam for 3 hours, 4 minutes, before their Champions League game versus Inter Milan. The team had to leave their bus, run 2km and travel to the ground by train. The team let in a goal in the first minute and lost the match 1–0.

For a country known for its bitterly cold climate in places, Russia is surprisingly a major force in beach football. In 2011, the Russian national team won the ultimate prize, the FIFA Beach Soccer World Cup, defeating Brazil 12–8 in the final.

LEV YASHIN was one of the first **GOALKEEPERS** to rush out of the goal and **INTERCEPT** the ball during attacks. He was also a deadly penalty stopper, saving more than **150 PENALTIES** during his career. In **1963**, he won the **BALLON D'OR AWARD** for the **WORLD'S BEST FOOTBALLER** – the only goalkeeper to receive the award.

Lena river

6. PERM

Zvezda 2005 Perm is the only team in the Russian Women's Football Championship to have won the competition three times in a row (2007–9). They also won in 2014 and 2015.

9. KHABAROVSK

FC SKA-Energiya's Lenin Stadium is Russia's most easterly professional football club, just 30km from the border with China. When Spartak Moscow drew them in the Russian Cup in 2016, players and supporters had to travel over 7,000km and put their watches forward seven hours.

7. TOMSK

The official mascot of the 2018 FIFA World Cup was designed by Ekaterina Bocharova, a graphic design student at Tomsk State University. Bocharova's design was Zabivaka, a wolf who wears sports glasses and whose name means 'the one who scores'.

The Leather Ball tournament celebrated its 50th anniversary in 2014. Each season, as many as 600,000 young footballers play for 40,000 different teams from all over Russia in Europe's biggest youth football competition.

8. VLADIVOSTOK

In 2006, three adventurous FC Zenit Saint Petersburg fans drove a staggering 8,000km across the country to see their team play FC Luch-Energiya in Vladivostok. The car broke down at their destination and they had to take a long, slow train home. Their club repaid their loyalty by presenting them with a brand new car!

CENTRAL ASIA

China is intent on becoming a world footballing power and its Super League clubs are signing star players from all around the world. China's national men's team played their first match in 1913 versus the Philippines and 87 years later recorded their biggest win, thrashing Guam 19-0, before making their World Cup debut two years later. The women's team have appeared at every Women's World Cup with the exception of 2011, when they did not qualify.

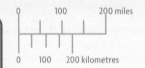

0 100 200 miles

0 100 200 kilometres

Despite playing their home matches on a pitch in front of thermal plant 4 – part of a giant power station – Erchim FC are Mongolia's most successful team. They have won the Mongolian Premier League ten times since 1996 as well as eight Mongolia Cup victories.

M O N

1. ÜRÜMQI

Xinjiang Tianshan Leopard FC are the most westerly team in both the Chinese Super League and League One. At more than 2,500km from the sea and over 3,000km from Beijing, fellow League One clubs have a 39-hour train journey or a long flight to play matches in the Xinjiang Sports Stadium.

Chinese footballer Liu Ailing appeared at three Women's World Cups, scoring eight goals. She also won a silver medal at the Olympic Games. Ailing was part of the Chinese team that reached the final of the 1999 Women's World Cup, where they lost narrowly to the USA.

10

C H I N A

HIMALAYAS

A forerunner of football over 2,500 years ago in China was called Cuju or Tsu Chu. A leather ball stuffed with bird feathers or animal hair had to be kicked through small, 30–40cm wide openings in a bamboo cane net. It was popular with wealthy nobles and was played by the founder of the Song Dynasty, Emperor Taizu.

Chan Yuen-ting became the world's first female coach to win a men's top-flight league championship when she coached Eastern to success in the 2015–6 Hong Kong Premier League. Eastern lost just two of their 16 games as they won their first league title in 21 years.

2. KUNMING

Regional airline Lucky Air got into the 2014 World Cup spirit with all its air stewardesses wearing Brazil shirts as they worked on flights. The stewardesses also organised World Cup quizzes on the flights.

XIE YUXIN became the first Chinese footballer to play for a **PROFESSIONAL CLUB** in Europe when he was signed by Dutch club **PEC ZWOLLE '82**, in 1987. Xie played more than **100 GAMES** for the Chinese national team and appeared at both the **1988 OLYMPICS** and the **1988 ASIAN CUP**.

EUROPE

ASIA

AFRICA

OCEANIA

Mekong river

BAY OF BENGAL

10. ERDENET

Khangarid are one of the very few teams outside the capital Ulaanbaatar to have won the Mongolian Premier League. Their most recent championship success was in 2010, despite winning only four games in the regular league season.

ULAANBAATAR ★

MONGOLIA

GOBI DESERT

9. SHENYANG

In a 2015 Chinese Super League game, a free-kick was taken very quickly by home side Liaoning Whowin. The opposing goalkeeper had left his goal to get a drink of water and Liaoning were able to roll the ball into the net unchallenged!.

8. DALIAN

Dalian Shide are the only Chinese team so far to go through an entire top league season unbeaten. This feat occurred in 1996 in the middle of an amazing spell for the club when they won seven out of nine league championships between 1992 and 2002.

BEIJING ★

Chinese TV channel LeTV provides live football commentary of UEFA Champions League games from Europe in the middle of the night. In one game in 2015, veteran reporter Dong Lu fell asleep at 5am in the morning and his snores could be heard over the air!

YELLOW SEA

6. NANCHONG

In 2016, Zhang Shuang managed to race 50m at China West Normal University with a football held between his legs while walking on his hands.

Yangtze river

5. SHANGHAI

In January 2017, the Chinese Super League's largest transfer deal was struck as Brazilian attacker Oscar moved to Shanghai SIPG for a record £60 million. He only took 34 minutes into his debut game to score his first goal.

7. TIANJIN

Divers took part in an underwater football match inside a fish aquarium at Haichang Polar Ocean World in 2014 as a stunt to mark the 2014 World Cup. Four divers with tanks and masks played a game on a pitch with small goals, with schools of fish for company.

★ TAIPEI

TAIWAN

PACIFIC OCEAN

3. QINGYUAN

With over 2,500 football students, the Evergrande Football School is the largest residential football academy in the world. The school features gyms, laboratories and 50 football pitches as well as a 13m-tall sculpture of the FIFA World Cup trophy.

4. HONG KONG

The Chinese women's football team, nicknamed the Steel Roses, won their first ever Asian Cup competition in 1986 when they beat Japan 2–0 in the final at Mong Kok Stadium. They beat Japan and Malaysia on the way to becoming champions.

SOUTH CHINA SEA

Model and Bollywood star John Abraham is co-owner of NorthEast United Football Club based in Guwahati, Assam. He played professionally in the Indian A-Division when he was younger, and is obsessed with making football as popular as cricket in India.

9. SIALKOT

This city in Pakistan has 200 factories that manufacture more than half of the world's hand-sewn footballs. In 2014, they produced 42 million footballs, which included all the Brazuca balls used at the FIFA World Cup.

AFGHANISTAN

★ KABUL

ISLAMABAD ★

10. JOGHORIE

In 2016, photos hit the Internet of a young boy, Murtaza Ahmadi, wearing a striped plastic bag to mimic the Argentina shirt of his idol, Lionel Messi. The publicity resulted in him receiving two real shirts and a football, all signed by Messi himself.

PAKISTAN

HIMALAYAS

NEPAL

KATHMANDU

NEW DELHI ★

India won the football tournament at the first Asian Games held in 1951 in New Delhi. The matches lasted 60 rather than 90 minutes, and the winning goal in the final versus Iran was scored by Indian striker Sahu Mewalal, the top scorer.

8. KARACHI

Pakistan's team won bronze in the 2014 Street Child World Cup in Rio, Brazil. All the children made the journey from Pakistan, where they had been homeless and living on the streets. Most of them did not have any documents or identity cards, but despite the difficulty they managed to get visas for Brazil.

Indus river

INDIA

6. CHANDANESWAR

In 2013, Manoj Mishra kept a ball balanced on his head as he rode his motorcycle 30km from Chandaneswar to Pichaboni in West Bengal. Three years later, he kept a ball balanced on his head as he walked 49.17km in just over 11 hours!

ARABIAN SEA

Godavari river

Most of the Indian national team that appeared at the 1948 and 1952 Olympics played in bare feet. This caused problems at the 1952 games where temperatures in the Finland stadium were below zero. After this match, the All-India Football Federation made wearing boots compulsory.

The biggest football derby in India is the clash between East Bengal and Asia's oldest surviving football club, Mohun Bagan, which was formed in 1889. In the 1997 derby at Salt Lake Stadium, a record 131,000 fans watched Baichung Bhutia score a hat-trick as East Bengal won 3–1.

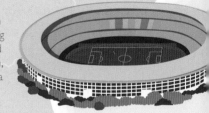

EUROPE

ASIA

AFRICA

OCEANIA

7. KOCHI

The Kerala Blasters were formed by Indian cricket legend, Sachin Tendulkar, in 2014 and that season made it to the final of the Indian Super League. The League features eight teams and one of the shortest seasons in world football, running from October to December each year.

SRI LANKA

★

INDIAN OCEAN

SRI JAYEWARDENEPURA KOTTE

5. PHUENTSHOLING

The Changlimithang Stadium looks more like a palace than a football ground and, in 2002, the Bhutan national football team recorded their first victory here. They had only three more wins at the ground over the next 15 years..

Football reached the Indian subcontinent, the southern region of Asia, for the first time in the 1870s. Today, it lags behind cricket as the region's most popular sport, but still attracts big crowds for important matches. With seven SAFF Championships and two Asian Games football titles, India is its most successful nation. This is a fascinating region of nations that have long histories and a passion for football. Thailand is traditionally the strongest national team with 14 Kings Cups — a competition mostly for teams in the region — and appearances at two Olympic Games.

BHUTAN

★ THIMPHU
5

Around 1,500 years old, Chinlone originated in Myanmar. It involves a team of players in a circle kicking a ball made from rattan canes woven together. Only the foot, heel and knee can be used to control the ball as players walk or dance round in the circle.

BANGLADESH

DHAKA ★

In 2015, at Dhaka Railway Station, Abdul Halim set an unusual world record for the fastest 100m on roller skates while successfully keeping a football balanced on his head!

MYANMAR (BURMA)

Irrawaddy river

Mekong river

VIETNAM

HANOI ★

LAOS

The Unusual Football Pitch Project squeezes odd-shaped football pitches into cramped spaces in built-up poor areas of Thailand's capital city, Bangkok, for local people to play on. Some of the pitches even go round corners!

BAY OF BENGAL

NAY PYI TAW ★

Salween river

4

★ VIENTIANE

SOUTH CHINA SEA

4. CHANG MAI

An unusual and unofficial World Cup competition took place here in 2014, featuring elephants as players! It's unclear who won, but the elephants could certainly thump the ball with their feet, although some cheated on occasion and carried the ball with their trunks!

Mekong river

THAILAND

★ BANGKOK

CAMBODIA

3. PRACHUAP KHIRI KHAN

This is the home town of Squadron Leader Piyapong Pue-on who scored over 250 goals for his club, Royal Thai Air Force. Pue-on won the Thai Premier League in 1997 as both a player and coach, and is Thailand's leading international goal scorer with 77 goals from 104 games.

3

PHNOM PENH ★

1

GULF OF THAILAND

ANDAMAN SEA

1. HO CHI MINH CITY

The Thống Nhất Stadium is home not only to two different clubs, Sài Gòn FC and Ho Chi Minh City, but also the Vietnamese women's national team. This team, nicknamed 'the Golden Girls', has won the AFF Women's Championship twice, in 2006 and 2012.

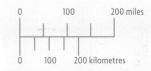

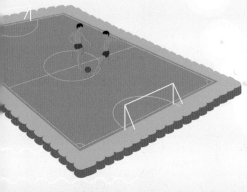

2. KOH PANYI

Islanders on Koy Panyi live in houses on stilts in the water. There was not enough land for a football pitch, so they built one that floats in the sea. There are no nets or barriers around the playing area, so if the ball leaves the pitch, players have to dive into the water to retrieve it.

0 — 100 — 200 miles

0 — 100 — 200 kilometres

EASTERN ASIA

Football is very popular in parts of this region. South Korea and its neighbour and rival, Japan, have strong professional leagues. South Korea's national team reached the semi-finals of the FIFA World Cup, won an Olympic bronze medal in 2012 and have been Asian Cup champions twice. Japan have won the Asian Cup four times, and their women's team were world champions in 2011.

North Korea became the first Asian team to reach the quarter-finals of the World Cup when Park Doo-Ik, a corporal in the North Korean army, scored the only goal in their shock 1966 win over Italy. The Italian team were pelted with rotten fruit and vegetables by disgruntled fans when they returned home!

Ri Myong-guk plays his club football with Pyongyang City and is the country's most capped player, appearing in goal for North Korea 79 times. His father and uncle also played in goal for the national team.

NORTH KOREA

PYONGYANG ★

KIM BYUNG-JI

wore a **NUMBER 700 SHIRT** when he played his **700TH MATCH** in Korean club football for the **JEONNAM DRAGONS** in 2015. At the age of 45, the goalkeeper became the **OLDEST PLAYER** ever in the **K-LEAGUE**. Back in 1998, playing for **ULSAN HYUNDAI**, Kim scored a **LAST-MINUTE HEADER** against Pohang Steelers and then saved **2 PENALTIES** in the shootout.

LEGEND!

1. PAJU CITY

This was the birthplace of Ahn Jung-hwan, whose goal at the 2002 World Cup knocked out Italy. He was playing football for an Italian club, Perugia, at the time and the chairman cancelled his contract saying he had 'ruined Italian football'.

SEOUL ★

SOUTH KOREA

YELLOW SEA

2. DAEGU

Fans had barely taken their seats in the Daegu World Cup Stadium in 2002, when the World Cup's fastest ever goal was scored. Turkey's Hakan Sükür scored after just 11 seconds to put Turkey ahead of South Korea, eventually winning 3–2.

EAST CHINA SEA

3. SEOGWIPO

The Jeju World Cup Stadium for the 2002 World Cup was built 14m below ground to avoid high winds. It is shaped like the mouth of a volcano and its roof resembles the fishing nets traditionally used in the region.

4. JEJU-DO ISLAND

South Korea's coach at the 2002 World Cup, Guus Hiddink, was given a free villa on this island after he led the team to become the first from Asia to reach the semi-finals of a World Cup. Hiddink was also rewarded with free flights for life with Korean Air.

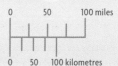

11. SAPPORO

The Sapporo Dome pitch is parked outside where the grass can catch the sun and grow. When needed, it slides inside the stadium, floating on a cushion of air like a hovercraft. The whole process takes less than two hours.

All top Japanese teams have cuddly and cute mascots – such as the Urawa Red Diamonds' four green wolves and Vissel Kobe's Movi the cow – to entertain fans. Many mascots learn their trade at the Choko Group mascot school in Tokyo.

SEA OF JAPAN (EAST SEA)

Hundreds of Japanese fans wore masks in honour of Tsuneyasu Miyamoto to Japan's matches after 2002.

10. SAITAMA

Japanese defender Tsuneyasu Miyamoto broke his nose in a training game just days before the 2002 World Cup. Undeterred, he played the opening game at Saitama wearing a protective mask that he painted black to make it more frightening!

7. NAGOYA

The first football World Cup for robots, RoboCup, kicked off in Nagoya in 1997. There were 39 teams entered and two winners in different leagues. Osaka University's Trackies won the medium-sized robot competition and CMUnited robots (below) won the small robot league.

In 2014, US president Barack Obama had a brief game of football . . . with a robot. ASIMO is a 1.3m-tall humanoid robot that can run at 9.6km/h, and kick and control a football.

PACIFIC OCEAN

JAPAN

9 ★ TOKYO

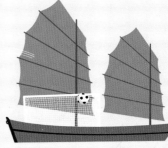

9. YOKOHAMA

In October 2011, the crowds at the Nippatsu Mitsuzawa Stadium saw an epic goal by Fagiano Okayama defender Ryujiro Ueda, from inside his team's own half of the pitch. His thumping header bounced and sailed over the head of the Yokohama FC goalkeeper. At 57.8m, this headed goal is one of the longest ever.

6. NARA

Before football in Japan, there was Kemari. Introduced from China, it saw players in traditional dress keep a ball made from deerskin in the air using any part of their body except their hands and arms. One of the first documented games in Japan took place in 644CE.

5. OITA

In 2013, Oita Trinita's goalkeeper, Keisuke Shimizu, accidentally helped score a goal against his own team. He tried to kick the ball up the pitch, but it bounced off the bottom of an opponent from Albirex Niigata, and ballooned over Shimizu's head into the net.

PACIFIC OCEAN

Seven of Japan's female footballers who won the 2011 Women's World Cup played for one club, INAC Kobe Leonessa. These included legendary attacking midfielder Homare Sawa, who first played for Japan in 1993 at the age of 15. She is the country's most capped player, with 205 matches in which she scored 89 goals.

8. SHIZUOKA CITY

This is the birthplace of the world's oldest professional footballer. Kazuyoshi Miura made his pro debut in 1986 and, in 2017, at the age of 50, was still playing and scoring goals. He played for Japan on 89 occasions between 1990 and 2000, scoring 55 goals, so he is also the country's second highest goal scorer.

Born in Baghdad, Emmanuel Baba Dawud, known as Ammo Baba, was a successful Iraqi player but an even more successful coach. He led Iraq to Gulf Cup victories in 1979, 1984 and 1988, an Arab Cup victory in 1988 and the Asian Games title in 1982. He also coached Iraq to qualify for the 1986 World Cup and two Olympic Games football tournaments in 1984 and 1988.

Euphrates river

Tigris river

SYRIA

LEBANON

BEIRUT ★

★ **DAMASCUS**

BAGHDAD ★

I R A Q

MEDITERRANEAN SEA

JERUSALEM ★ ★ **AMMAN**

ISRAEL

JORDAN

KUWAI

KUWAIT CI

4. HA'IL

This is the home of legendary Saudi Arabian goalkeeper Mohamed Al-Deayea. Including friendlies, Al-Deayea played 181 times for his country. When he retired in 2007, a special match between his club Al-Hilal and Italian side, Juventus was held at the King Fahd Stadium in Riyadh. It was attended by more than 70,000 fans.

4

RIYADH ★

Saeed Al-Owairan played for Riyadh-based club Al-Shabab throughout his career, and scored more than 200 goals. At the 1994 World Cup, he ran 70m with the ball to score a goal against Belgium and was named 1994 Asian Footballer of the Year. He received a free Rolls Royce car as a reward when he returned to Saudi Arabia.

With open space rare in the densely built-up Gaza settlement bordering the Mediterranean Sea, a pitch was built on the rooftop of an apartment building in 2015. It is the Middle East's first rooftop football ground.

RED SEA

3

3. JEDDAH

Al-Ittihad was formed in 1929, making it Saudi Arabia's oldest football club. It was also the first to win back-to-back AFC Champions League competitions in 2004 and 2005. The club, which plays at the 62,241-capacity King Abdullah Sports City Stadium, underwent quite a few changes in recent years, with four different managers in 2011 and another four in 2014.

S A

R

★ **SANA'A**

Y E M E N

Hapoel Be'er Sheva of Israel is the only top club in the Middle East owned by a woman, Alona Barkat. She bought the club in 2007 when they played in the Israeli second division, and in 2016 celebrated winning the first Israeli Premier League championship in 40 years.

2

GULF OF ADE

CASPIAN SEA

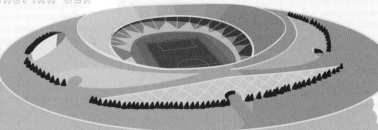

★ TEHRAN

The Azadi Stadium is home to two of Iran's leading football clubs, Persepolis FC and Esteghlal FC, but its biggest ever crowd was for an Iran versus Australia play-off to decide which team would appear at the 1998 World Cup. In front of 128,000 people, Iran went through on the away goals rule.

The Middle East includes nations of all sizes, but they all contain many ardent football fans. In 2010, it was announced that Qatar would become the smallest nation ever to host the FIFA World Cup and the first in the Middle East to do so. Because of the extremely hot climate in summer, it will also be the first World Cup that has been moved to the northern hemisphere's winter months of November and December.

During a 2013 Kuwait League match between Al-Nasr and Al-Arabi, referee Saad al-Fadhi lost his temper. He awarded a penalty against Al-Nasr, but then was jostled by the players. The referee punched Al-Nasr player Abdulaziz Farraj, then showed him a red card!

Iran's football kit for the 2014 World Cup featured a large print of the Asiatic cheetah on the shirts. This was to highlight how critically endangered the creature is, with under 100 thought to be living in the wild, all in Iran.

0   100   200 miles

0   100   200 kilometres

I R A N

PERSIAN GULF

The owner of the Abu Dhabi-based Al-Jazira Sports & Culture Club, Sheikh Mansour, also owns three foreign football clubs each with 'City' in their title: Melbourne City in Australia, New York City in the United States and Manchester City in England.

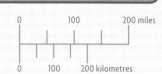

★ MANAMA

HRAIN

★ DOHA
QATAR

1

GULF OF OMAN

★ ABU DHABI

D
B I A
I A

★ MUSCAT

U A E

1. KHOR FAKKAN

A street in this remote town is named Hurriyya, meaning 'Freedom', in honour of the UAE's most famous football fan, restaurant owner Khaled Al-Hammadi. He has faithfully followed the national team everywhere since 1974 and always carries a large megaphone to cheer on his side.

The world's largest football is on display in Doha. It was unveiled by the Doha Bank in 2013, has a diameter of 12.19m and weighs a whopping 960kg. This beat the record held in Muscat, Oman, for a ball made the previous year, which measured 10.08m and weighed 750kg.

O M A N

ARABIAN SEA

ALI DAEI is Iran's most capped player, with **149 APPEARANCES**, and the **WORLD'S LEADING INTERNATIONAL GOAL SCORER**. Between 1993 and 2006, Daei scored **109 GOALS** for his country. Daei studied **MATERIALS ENGINEERING** at university and is now both a **CLUB COACH** and owner of **DAEI SPORT**, a company that makes football kits, including the **IRANIAN NATIONAL TEAM** strip.

. MOKHA

With land travel out of their country blocked by conflict in 2015, the Yemen national team braved rough seas to sail by wooden boat from the port of Mokha to the African nation of Djibouti. They were then able to fly to Qatar, where they have played their international matches since 2010.

ASIA

OCEANIA

ANTARCTICA

OCEANIA

TIMOR SEA

AUSTRALIA

INDIAN
OCEAN

GREAT
AUSTRALIAN
BIGHT

The smallest footballing region, Oceania, is formed of several larger countries – Australia, Papua New Guinea and New Zealand – and lots of smaller island nations spread across the Pacific Ocean. Seeking more competition, Australia switched to playing its football matches in Asia in 2006. However, some Oceanian players and one New Zealand-based team, the Wellington Phoenix, compete in Australia's leading club competition, the A-League.

The Oceania Football Confederation (OFC) has run football in the region since 1966 and is now made up of 11 full members and 3 associates (junior members). Despite difficulties in staging competitions due to finances and the big distances between countries, football continues to excite and entertain in this region.

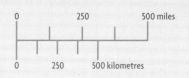

BISMARCK
SEA

PAPUA NEW GUINEA

SOLOMON ISLANDS

TUVALU

SOLOMON SEA

CORAL SEA

VANUATU

FIJI

NEW CALEDONIA
Part of France

TONGA

SOUTH PACIFIC OCEAN

TASMAN SEA

NEW ZEALAND

PAPUA NEW GUINEA

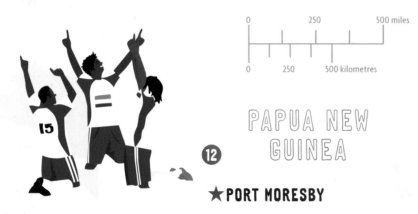

★ **PORT MORESBY**

12. LAE

The Lae City Dwellers were only formed as a football club in 2014, but the following year they won the country's top competition, the National Soccer League. They repeated this feat in 2016, when both of their goals in the final game were scored by Raymond Gunemba, the first directly from a corner.

During the 2015 Asian Cup, held in Australia, 12-year-old ball boy Stephen White became a hero in China during their national team's match versus Saudi Arabia. Facing a penalty, Chinese goalkeeper Wang Dalei asked Stephen which way to go, followed his advice to dive left and saved the penalty.

AUSTRALIA AND PAPUA NEW GUINEA

Australia's first known football match took place in 1880 and was between Wanderers and King's School of Parramatta. There have been plenty of matches since, however, with the men's national team, known as the Socceroos, winning the Asian Cup in 2015, five years after the women's team, the Matildas, achieved the same feat.

Ray Richards was selected for Australia's 1974 FIFA World Cup squad, but was booked three times during Australia's match with Chile. He continued playing until the referee, Jafar Namdar from Iran, finally noticed and sent him off the pitch!

Perth Glory play football in Australia's top club competition, the A-League. Located on the western coast of Australia, the team have to travel 2,700km just to play their nearest rival, Adelaide United.

1. MOUNT HAWTHORN

The male football club Floreat Athena FC appointed Italian female football legend Carolina Morace as their Technical Director in 2015. Morace scored 105 goals for the Italian national women's team and went on to coach the Perth Glory women's football team.

TIM CAHILL played for **SYDNEY OLYMPIC** and **SYDNEY UNITED YOUTH** teams before a career with teams including **MILLWALL** and **EVERTON** in England and the **NEW YORK RED BULLS** in the USA. He is Australia's leading goal scorer with **48 GOALS** in **97 GAMES**, and the only player from the Asian Football Confederation (AFC) to score goals at **3 FIFA WORLD CUPS** in a row.

2. PERTH

The A-League is a ten-team competition, and goalkeeper Liam Reddy had already played for seven of the sides when he joined Perth Glory from Western Sydney Wanderers in 2016.

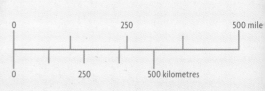

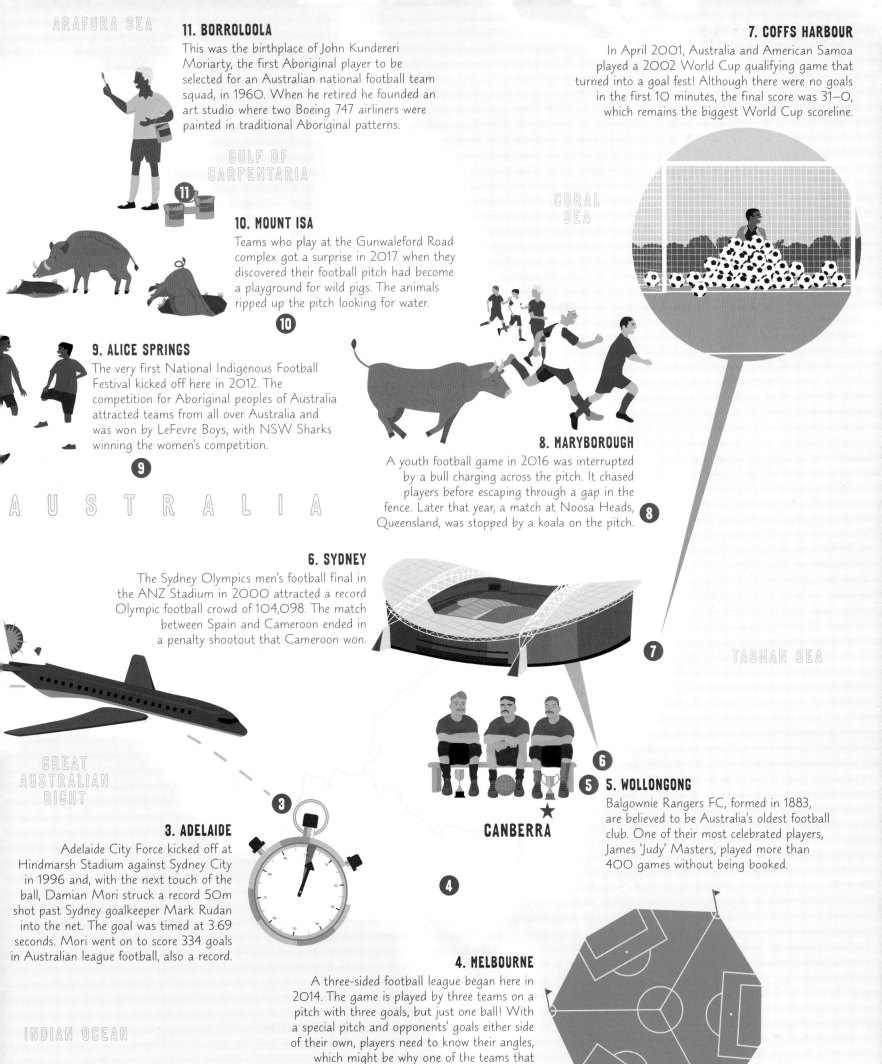

11. BORROLOOLA

This was the birthplace of John Kundereri Moriarty, the first Aboriginal player to be selected for an Australian national football team squad, in 1960. When he retired he founded an art studio where two Boeing 747 airliners were painted in traditional Aboriginal patterns.

7. COFFS HARBOUR

In April 2001, Australia and American Samoa played a 2002 World Cup qualifying game that turned into a goal fest! Although there were no goals in the first 10 minutes, the final score was 31–0, which remains the biggest World Cup scoreline.

10. MOUNT ISA

Teams who play at the Gunwaleford Road complex got a surprise in 2017 when they discovered their football pitch had become a playground for wild pigs. The animals ripped up the pitch looking for water.

9. ALICE SPRINGS

The very first National Indigenous Football Festival kicked off here in 2012. The competition for Aboriginal peoples of Australia attracted teams from all over Australia and was won by LeFevre Boys, with NSW Sharks winning the women's competition.

8. MARYBOROUGH

A youth football game in 2016 was interrupted by a bull charging across the pitch. It chased players before escaping through a gap in the fence. Later that year, a match at Noosa Heads, Queensland, was stopped by a koala on the pitch.

6. SYDNEY

The Sydney Olympics men's football final in the ANZ Stadium in 2000 attracted a record Olympic football crowd of 104,098. The match between Spain and Cameroon ended in a penalty shootout that Cameroon won.

3. ADELAIDE

Adelaide City Force kicked off at Hindmarsh Stadium against Sydney City in 1996 and, with the next touch of the ball, Damian Mori struck a record 50m shot past Sydney goalkeeper Mark Rudan into the net. The goal was timed at 3.69 seconds. Mori went on to score 334 goals in Australian league football, also a record.

5. WOLLONGONG

Balgownie Rangers FC, formed in 1883, are believed to be Australia's oldest football club. One of their most celebrated players, James 'Judy' Masters, played more than 400 games without being booked.

4. MELBOURNE

A three-sided football league began here in 2014. The game is played by three teams on a pitch with three goals, but just one ball! With a special pitch and opponents' goals either side of their own, players need to know their angles, which might be why one of the teams that compete is called Athletico Geometry!

CANBERRA

ARAFURA SEA

GULF OF CARPENTARIA

CORAL SEA

AUSTRALIA

TASMAN SEA

GREAT AUSTRALIAN BIGHT

INDIAN OCEAN

NEW ZEALAND

Although this country is probably more famous for the All Blacks rugby union team, football is played widely in New Zealand, and there are both men's and women's national leagues. The game was first played in the 1880s, and the men's national team, the All Whites, played their first full international against rivals and neighbours Australia in 1922. The women's national team was founded in 1975 and is known as the Football Ferns.

2. NAPIER

The Awatoto Public Course is one of nine FootGolf courses in New Zealand. This hybrid of golf and football sees players kick a regular-sized football off the tee and try to get the ball into an oversized golf hole in as few kicks as possible. The game began in the Netherlands in 2008.

PACIFIC OCEAN

ASIA

OCEANIA

ANTARCTICA

NEW ZEALAND

NORTH ISLAND

SOUTH ISLAND

TASMAN SEA

★ WELLINGTON

1. AUCKLAND

North Harbour Stadium hosted the 2010 Women's Soccer Oceania Championship in which the four top scorers were all New Zealanders. Amber Hearn scored in every game of the tournament. She is also New Zealand's all-time leading scorer with 50 goals in 109 matches.

New Zealand's most-capped footballer, Abby Erceg, made her debut for the full national team at the age of 16. By the end of 2016, she had played 129 full national team games, was the team's captain, and had played club football for teams in Germany, Spain and the United States.

New Zealand's oldest and most important cup competition, the Chatham Cup, is named after a British warship, *HMS Chatham*, whose crew donated a cup, costing £175, in 1922. The Jack Batty Cup is awarded to the best player in the final and is named after a sailor on *HMS Chatham*, who won it three times (1924, 1929, 1931).

Wellington Phoenix's most ardent supporters, the Yellow Fever, have an official website, T-shirts and even a nightclub they meet in after games! They also organise the New Zealand Freestyle Football Championships for footballers able to perform all sorts of imaginative moves.

3. CANTERBURY

One of the first known organised women's matches between regions of New Zealand was held here in 1921 when a local team played one from Wellington, the Aotea Ladies, who wore gym dresses. At the time, some people in New Zealand believed that it was 'dangerous' and 'unladylike' for women to play.

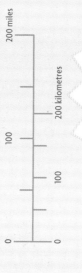

4. DUNEDIN

Southern United are the most southerly top football club in Oceania and play their matches in the Forsyth Barr Stadium. The giant clear plastic roof and sides measure 20,500m^2 – about 80 times the size of a tennis court. Rainwater is collected from the roof to water the grass.

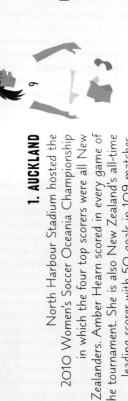

200 miles

200 kilometres

100

100

0

0

Wellington-born **WYNTON ALAN WHAI RUFER** was the youngest member of the **ALL WHITES** at the **1982 WORLD CUP**. He went on to play for **NORWICH CITY** in England, Switzerland's **FC ZURICH** and German teams **WERDER BREMEN** and **KAISERSLAUTERN**. He scored over **220 LEAGUE GOALS** and won **3 OCEANIA FOOTBALLER OF THE YEAR** awards (1989, 1990, 1992).

THE PACIFIC ISLANDS

Scattered throughout the Pacific Ocean, these island nations, along with New Zealand and Papua New Guinea, make up the Oceania Football Confederation (OFC). Its 11 full members and associate member islands take part in a range of competitions, including the OFC Nations Cup for national teams and the OFC Champions League for leading club sides.

6. TAHITI

The 2013 FIFA Beach Soccer World Cup was held at Tahua To'atā Stadium in Papeete and saw an incredible 243 goals scored in 32 matches (an average of 7.59 goals per game).

PACIFIC OCEAN

HAWAII (USA)

1. BAIRIKI

The Bairiki National Stadium is the home of Kiribati's national team, but no international games can be played there because the pitch is made of sand, not grass. Since their first game in 1979, all the team's matches have been played away from home.

COOK ISLANDS

4. BA

The Battle of the Giants is a major football competition held every year on Fiji for the top ten regions or clubs. Ba FC have won the competition a record 16 times and are one of the few football teams to play in all-black socks, shorts and shirts.

AMERICAN SAMOA

SAMOA

TUVALU

TONGA   NIUE

MARSHALL ISLANDS

KIRIBATI

NAURU

FIJI

VANUATU

NEW CALEDONIA (FRANCE)

3. SUVA

Suva was the first port of call for the New Zealand team when they began a long-distance fight to qualify for the 1982 World Cup in Spain. The squad flew to China, Kuwait, Indonesia and Saudi Arabia as they played 15 matches and travelled 88,000km – equivalent to more than twice around the world!

NORTHERN MARIANA (USA)

GUAM (USA)

MICRONESIA

PALAU

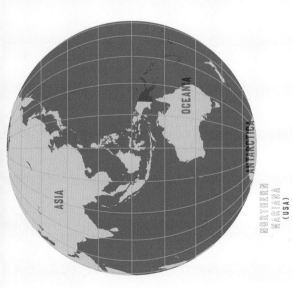

OCEANIA

ASIA

ANTARCTICA

PAPUA NEW GUINEA

PORT MORESBY ★

SOLOMON ISLANDS

HONIARA ★

The OFC Nations Cup, competed for by national teams in Oceania, was held in Honiara, the capital of the Solomon Islands, in 2013.

2. VANUATU

Vanuatu's under-23 team are known as the Vanuatu Cyclone, and they certainly swept through one of their opponents at the 2015 Pacific Games. The team hammered the Federated States of Micronesia 46–0! Jean Kaltack scored 16 goals.

5. MATAVERA

The training base for the Cook Islands' national team is here. They have finished as runners-up in the Polynesia Cup twice (1998, 2000), which is amazing considering that the population of under 25,000 is spread out across islands that cover an area about the size of Western Europe.

FRENCH POLYNESIA

RAPA NUI (EASTER ISLAND)

0   250   500 miles
0 250 500 kilometres

USA

The shirts of the US women's national team feature three stars, one for each of the FIFA Women's World Cups that the team have won.

CHILE

Chile's most successful club, Colo-Colo, are named after a famous 16th-century Mapuche native South American chief. The club has won the Chilean league more than 30 times.

NORTH POLE

In 2001, three ships moored near the North Pole staged a tournament. The matches were played on ice and featured teams from the crews of the *Oden* from Sweden, the *Healy* from the USA and Germany's *Polarstern*. The Germans won.

90
EXTRA

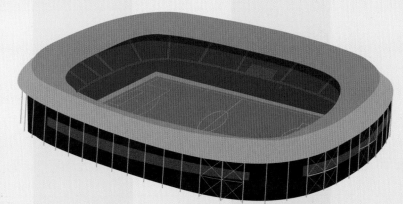

NETHERLANDS

Rotterdam's De Kuip Stadium was the location of Luxembourg's 2–1 win over the Netherlands in 1963, a qualifying match for the 1964 European Championship. This victory was Luxembourg's last in qualifying until 1995.

FINLAND

Helsingin Jalkapalloklubi (known as HJK) are Finland's most successful football club. They have won Finland's top league, the Veikkausliiga, 27 times.

ECUADOR

Ecuador's head coach Dušan Drašković spent six years (1988–93) driving around the country in a battered old car to find youngsters playing in streets, fields and on hillsides. At the 2002 World Cup, 19 of the 22-man Ecuador squad had been found by the coach.

MOZAMBIQUE

Famous track athlete Maria Mutola won an Olympic gold medal in the 800m in 2000 and 10 World Championship athletic titles. In 2011, she played her first match for the Mozambique women's national football team, a 1–0 win over Swaziland.

INDIA

The biggest football derby in India is the clash between East Bengal and Asia's oldest surviving football club, Mohun Bagan, which was formed in 1889. In the 1997 derby at Salt Lake Stadium, Kolkata, a record 131,000 fans watched Bhaichung Bhutia score a hat-trick. East Bengal won 3–1.

ITALY

In a 1989 match between Pianta and Arpax, Italian striker Fernando d'Ercoli was shown the red card by the referee and was so angry he grabbed the card and ate it!

FRANCE

Defender Franck Jurietti proudly made his debut for the French national team at the Stade de France in 2005 against Cyprus. He came on with only five seconds of the game to play and never played for his country again, making it one of the shortest international careers ever!

ANTARCTICA

In 2015, English player David Beckham flew from Argentina to Antarctica on board a Russian plane to play on the ice of Antarctica's Union glacier with staff from the nearby science station. The chilly seven-a-side game ended in a 3–3 draw.

1. In which North African country was a record-breaking footballer born?

2. Between which countries did the 'Football War' take place in 1970?

3. In which Middle Eastern city is the world's largest football on display?

4. In which US city was America's youngest professional footballer signed by DC United at just 14 years of age?

5. In which Asian country was the ancient game of Kemari first documented in 644ce?

6. In which country did elephants play a World Cup competition game in 2014?

7. In which large Asian country did divers take part in an underwater football match in 2014?

WHERE IN THE WORLD?

So you think you know all about football and footballers? Why not take this global challenge to recall the locations of some of the extraordinary feats, incredible events and curious rituals that you have discovered in this book. If you can get more than half of the questions correct without peeking at the answers at the bottom of the right-hand page, then you are an *Atlas of Football Champ!*

8. In which European country did brothers play against each other in the 2016 UEFA European Championship?

9. Which Swiss stadium can only be reached via cable car?

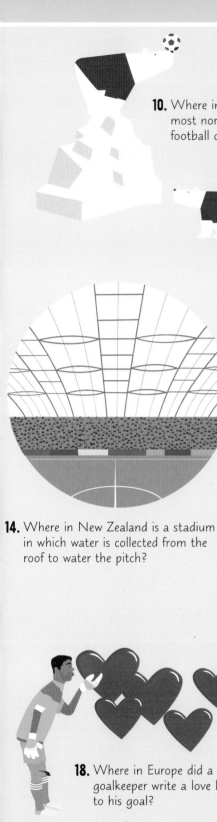

10. Where in Scandinavia is the most northerly professional football club in the world?

11. In which city did Russia's first-ever public museum of football open in 2007?

12. In which Oceanic country was a match interrupted by a charging bull in 2016?

13. In which UK city could fans buy a toilet seat in the club colours?

14. Where in New Zealand is a stadium in which water is collected from the roof to water the pitch?

15. For which North American country did Janine Beckie play when she scored the fastest goal in Olympic women's football?

16. Where in eastern Africa does superfan Isaac Juma Onyango support his team?

17. In which South American country did a 19-year-old win a competition to design the national football kit?

18. Where in Europe did a goalkeeper write a love letter to his goal?

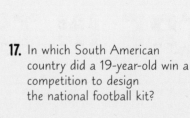

19. In which town is Spain's oldest football club, founded in 1889?

20. In which South African city was the world's most expensive football made?

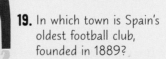

GLOSSARY

AFC Asian Football Confederation, the governing body of sport in Asia.

A-League Australia's top club competition.

ANAPROF Asociación Nacional Pro Fúbol, until 2009 the top league in Panama.

attacker Any player who plays the ball forward towards the opposing team's goal to try and score.

away game A game played at an opposing team's ground.

back pass A pass that a player makes back towards their goalkeeper; a defensive move.

ball boy A young person, male or female, stationed around the edge of the pitch whose role is to help retrieve balls that go out of play.

beach football A variant of association football that is played on a beach or on sand.

bicycle kick A move in which a player jumps in the air to kick the ball back over their head.

CAF Confederation of African Football, the governing body of the sport in Africa.

capped Describes someone who has appeared as a player for a national team; they earn one cap for each appearance.

CECAFA Council for East and Central Africa Football Associations, an association of football-playing nations in East and Central Africa.

clean sheet When a goalkeeper or team does not let in a single goal during a match.

coach The person who trains the players of a team.

CONCACAF Confederation of North, Central American and Caribbean Association Football, the governing body of the sport in North and Central America and the Caribbean.

CONMEBOL Confederaçao Suldamericana de Futebol, the governing body of the sport in South America.

COSAFA Council of Southern Africa Football Associations.

debut A player's first appearance for a team.

defender A player whose main role is to try and stop the opposing team's attackers from scoring a goal.

derby A match between two, usually local, rivals.

equalise Describes when a goal makes the score even.

EURO European football.

extra time An additional period of time, normally two halves of 15 minutes, which helps to decide the winner if the score is tied.

FIFA Fédération Internationale de Football Association, the world governing body for the game of association football since 1904. FIFA established the World Cup.

final The last game in a competition between teams.

first division The highest league competition for clubs in many countries.

free kick A kick awarded to a player of one team when a player in the other has committed a foul; the player kicks a stationary ball without any opposing players within 10 yards.

goalkeeper The player who guards the goal; he is allowed to control the ball with his hands inside the goal area.

half time The break between the two halves of a game, usually lasting 15 minutes.

hat-trick Three or more goals scored in a game by a single player.

header The striking of a ball in the air by a player's head.

home game A game played at a team's own ground.

I-League The Indian professional league for men's association football clubs.

keepy-uppy The skill of juggling a football to keep it off the ground using the feet, knees, chest, shoulders or head.

kit The clothing worn by players that is specific to their team.

league A competition between clubs that accumulate points over a series of matches.

logo A symbol or design used by clubs to identify their kit and other products.

manager The official in charge of the day-to-day running of the team.

mascot	An animal, person or thing adopted by a team that is supposed to bring good luck.	save	When a goalkeeper prevents the football from crossing the goal line.
match	A football game.	season	The time of year when the main competitions in a particular country are played.
midfielder	A player who links play between attackers and defenders.	second division	A section of the league below the first division. Teams who finish at the top of this division at the end of the season are often promoted into the top division.
MLS	Major League Soccer, the professional men's soccer league in the USA.		
NASL	North American Soccer League, a professional men's soccer league with eight teams: six in the USA, one in Canada and one in Puerto Rico.	squad	A club or national team's group of players from which the coach or manager will select a number to form the team for a match.
NWSL	National Women's Soccer League, a professional women's soccer league in the USA.	stadium	A sports ground with tiers of seats for spectators.
OFC	Oceania Football Confederation, the governing body of the sport in Oceania.	stand	The traditional standing area for spectators in a sports stadium.
outfield	Any player other than the goalkeeper.	striker	A front-running central attacker, with the main role of scoring goals.
pass	When a player kicks the ball to one of their own team.	strip	The identifying outfit worn by a team's players.
penalty	This kick is awarded when a foul or deliberate handball is committed inside the penalty area. A penalty is taken by one player who is opposed only by the goalkeeper.	studs	Small points on the underneath of a player's boots that help grip the ground and stop the player from slipping.
pitch	The field of play.	substitute	A player who is brought onto the pitch during a match in exchange for another player.
play-off	A series of matches that decide whether clubs are promoted or relegated near the end of a season. In some leagues, play-offs decide who is that season's champions.	table football	A tabletop version of football played with miniature figures of players.
Premier League	The top division of club football in some countries.	team	A group of players forming one side in a competitive sport.
professional	A player who has signed to a club and is paid a wage.	trainers	Soft sports shoes used by players.
qualifier	A match that is part of a competition which determines which teams can take part in a major tournament such as the World Cup.	transfer	Describes the action taken when a player under contract moves between clubs; it describes the moving of the player's registration from one association club to another.
red card	This is given to a player when they have committed a serious offence or have been issued with two yellow cards in the same game. The red card is held up by the referee to signal that a player is to be sent off; the player is not replaced.	trophy	A cup or other impressive object awarded as a prize for victory in a match.
		UEFA	Union of European Football Associations, the governing body of the sport in Europe.
referee	The official who is in charge of the game.	World Cup	The international football competition held by FIFA every four years between the top national teams in the world.
rollersoccer	A variant of football played on roller skates.		
SAFF	South Asian Football Federation, a group of football-playing nations in South Asia.	yellow card	This is held up by a referee to signal a caution for a minor offence.

INDEX

CAERLEON

2/6/18